Comments regar

"Good News for ... ilies who are looking ... ds of children of all a... from Bible stories to current events to sports history. Readers and hearers are encouraged to think deeply about the questions that follow each thought. Answers are given too, so readers are not left in doubt. I love this book! It is simple without being condescending, profound without being preachy, and both biblical and practical. Great family resource!"
Dr. Laura Mae Gardner,
International Personnel Consultant & Trainer,
Wycliffe International and SIL

"Along with embracing the words of Luke, Bryan incorporates stories from his own life and ministry which present in practical ways compelling truths from this gospel writer. This book proves to be not only a source of encouragement, but an easy-to-use resource for those who seek to deepen and enrich their relationship with Jesus Christ. *Good News for the Family* is exactly that—good news which will undoubtedly lay a solid foundation for the Christian family as together they explore God's Word."
Joe Dabrowski,
Lead Pastor, First Baptist Church of Okemos,
Okemos, MI

"First, what a great little book for families. You have done an amazing job, not only with this one on Luke, but also the one from Proverbs. We work with a group of young families in our local church, and I think this book would be a great resource for them as they seek to share God's truth with their kids. So, nice work! I can see this book being used around the kitchen table at meals, or when a child is headed to bed. The short readings give the parents opportunity to also talk them over with their kids."
Perry Bradford,
Director, Barnabas International,
Rockford, IL

"Do you ever feel guilty for not having family Bible time? Do you lack confidence to attempt the same? Bryan Coupland has done it again. Like his previous volume from Proverbs he has provided a user-friendly, self-guided, full-featured, Bible based family devotional tool from the gospel according to Luke. It is so useable that it eliminates the excuse of any parent or leader to opt out based on ignorance of the Bible, or lack of experience in leading Bible discussions. Because it covers the entire book of Luke it provides a default by-product of enhancing "biblical literacy.' Participants learn life-changing truths in their biblical context. Most importantly, Bryan writes from a personal experience of these life-changing truths expressed in a real and relevant manner. My only regret is that we did not have this when our children were younger and still at home. We need one of these for every book of the Bible."
*Brad Stephenson,*
*Lead Pastor,*
*Deltona Alliance Church,*
*Deltona, FL*

"Well-organized; nice flow of material. Very clear; easy to follow. Material covered in an excellent way; good themes chosen that meet kids "right where they are," helping them deal with challenges and issues of life. Written in a way that is easy for kids to understand, yet fitting for adults as well; simplifies some of the more difficult passages and presents/explains them in ways that kids can comprehend…and thus apply. *Good News for the Family* was written in a way that encourages good parent/child interaction and family discussion. Thoughtful questions will cause the reader to think about the material shared. I've worked with quite a few families in my counseling practice and can wholeheartedly recommend this book as part of their family devotions. This book is helpful for children of all ages as well as adults."
*Ruth Ann Graybill,*
*Therapist/Clinical Social Worker,*
*Biola Counseling Center, Biola University,*
*La Mirada, CA*

# Good News for the Family

## 100 Devotionals from the Gospel of Luke

*With Questions and Answers*

*Bryan R. Coupland.*
*Isaiah 41:10*

# Bryan R. Coupland

Spring Glen Publishing • Debary, Florida 32753-0751
www.SpringGlenPublishing.com

# GOOD NEWS FOR THE FAMILY

Copyright © 2012 by Bryan R. Coupland. All rights reserved.
Published by:  Spring Glen Publishing
              Box 530751
              Debary, Florida   32753-0751

Unless otherwise indicated, Bible quotations are taken from the NEW AMERICAN STANDARD BIBLE. Copyright © 1960, 1962, 1963, 1968, 1971, 1972, 1973, 1975, 1977, 1995 by the Lockman Foundation. Used by permission.

Scripture taken from THE AMPLIFIED BIBLE, Old Testament copyright © 1965, 1987, by the Zondervan Corporation. The Amplified New Testament copyright © 1958, 1987 by The Lockman Foundation. Used by permission.

Verses marked KJV are taken from the King James Version.

No part of this publication may be reproduced, stored in a retrieval system, or transmitted in any form or by any means, except for quotations in printed reviews, without the prior permission of the publisher.

ISBN – 978-0-9831235-2-1
LCCN – 2012901282

Cover – *www.designbystacy.com*
Back cover photo – *http://PhotoInspiration.weebly.com*

1. Family   2. Devotionals   3. Raising children   4. Bible study

Printed and bound in the United States of America.

## DEDICATION

The author would like to dedicate this book to his parents, Garnet and Esmee Coupland.

It's unfortunate that while we're growing up, we don't fully appreciate the qualities and values—even the world view—that our parents are hoping to instill in us. We're very conscious of the rules, the discipline, and the chores we're forced to submit to, without understanding the loving motives behind them.

When I look in the rear-view mirror now, I understand and appreciate my parents' unwavering adherence to the principles of biblical Christianity, hard work, honesty, patriotism, and a balanced blend of frugality and generosity.

I am deeply grateful to my parents and pray that I have passed these same values on to our three children who will in turn pass them on to our grandchildren.

# FOREWORD

Our church family is always looking for ways to strengthen the family. A year or so ago our congregation was involved in a special emphasis on "the home," teaching some courses, sponsoring a family-related seminar, and instructing our parents on ways of teaching and training their own children in the things of the Lord. Throughout this process, our leadership sought resources that would aid the parents within our flock to raise their children for Christ. We were struggling, however, to find just the right material to use for family instruction. While some Christian leaders recommend a catechism for such purposes, we wanted something that would draw more precisely from Scripture and engage the children directly in the Word of God. That is when Bryan Coupland's first book *Growing a Wise Family - 100 Devotionals from the Book of Proverbs* found its way into my study and our search was over. As the title of that volume suggests, the book is developed around 100 proverbs, each to be used in family instruction. Each proverb is explained and well-illustrated by the author. At the end of each study, three well-chosen, age-appropriate discussion questions are provided. The author then offers suggested answers to each question. A number of our families made excellent use of Mr. Coupland's first book.

When I learned that Bryan would be providing a sequel to his family devotional on Proverbs with one on the life of Christ, drawn straight from the Gospel of Luke, I was enthusiastic. I was excited first because another resource for family devotions would be available from Bryan's able pen and because many of our people have gone through the first book more than once. But even more, I love the topic. There is nothing more important in the life of a believer than Jesus Christ. In a day when evangelical authors and speakers emphasize topics like thanksgiving, finding purpose, service, or even the church, it's easy to really miss the point of the Christian life which is Christ. Our lives are to be Christ-centered, Christ-driven, and Christ-focused. Our peace with God begins when we come to Christ by faith alone. Our spiritual growth comes only as we follow Christ. Our hopes and dreams are centered on Christ. Our true needs are met in Christ. Our eternal destiny is with Christ. As Paul references the coming again of the Lord, he speaks of "Christ, who is our life" (Colossians 3:4). In the face of death, the apostle had no fear for he wrote, "For to me, to live is Christ and to die is gain" (Philippians 1:21). He counted all things as rubbish for the sake of Christ (Philippians 3:7, 8), in order that he might gain Christ (3:8), have Christ's righteousness (3:9), and that he might know Christ (3:10).

In other words, the Christian experience is all about Christ. Where better to learn about Him than in the Gospels, and Luke is unsurpassed, even in the Gospels, in informing us about the life of Jesus Christ. Bryan has made a wise choice in helping us raise wise families. There is nothing better, nothing more glorious, nothing more practical than to teach our young ones about Christ. This excellent book will do that very thing.

As you read *Good News for the Family*, you will find that Bryan Coupland writes well. He is interesting, biblical, and creative. I found his book easy to use and of real value. He wrote the book with ten to thirteen-year-olds in mind, but the material can be easily adapted to younger or older children. For those looking for an aid to help teach their children the Word of God and engage them in the things of Christ, *Good News for the Family* is an excellent choice. Enjoy!

Dr. Gary Gilley,
Author and Senior Pastor,
Southern View Chapel,
Springfield, IL

# INTRODUCTION TO PARENTS

The gospel of Luke has been called the most beautifully written account of the life and ministry of Jesus Christ. It begins with the angel's announcement to Mary that she will give birth to the incarnate Son of God, and ends with His post-resurrection return to His heavenly Father's side.

Tradition tells us that Luke was a Gentile, possibly from Antioch of Syria. We know that he was a doctor because the apostle Paul calls him "the beloved physician" (Colossians 4:14). If, in fact, Luke was a Gentile, then the Holy Spirit chose him as the only non-Jew to write a book of the Bible.

Since Luke wrote his gospel around AD 61-62, he penned it about three decades after Christ's crucifixion, burial, resurrection, and ascension. Like the apostle Paul, Luke was not an eye-witness of Christ's ministry on earth. However, as you would expect from a doctor, he diligently gathered details from those who had walked the roads from Nazareth to Jerusalem with Jesus. To give these facts a historical context, Luke included the names of governors and Roman emperors, as if to guide any historians more accurately.

Luke is also credited with writing the book of Acts, and we learn from a number of verses there that he was a missionary companion of the apostle Paul. These are called the "we passages" since Luke refers to Paul and himself as missionary companions (Acts 16:10; 2 Timothy 4:11).

Luke addresses a man by the name of Theophilus early in his gospel (Luke 1:3). Who is he and why is Luke writing him? There is no definite answer to either question, but it seems from Luke's salutation that he was a man of wealth and high social status. The beloved physician wanted him to learn the correct details of Jesus' life so he could grow spiritually. The Holy Spirit obviously wanted the Church to also have this detailed record.

Some of the themes Luke emphasizes in his gospel are:
- Jesus' concern for those looked down on by others: the poor (21:2); the diseased (5:12); the Gentiles i.e. Samaritans (10:33); the sinner (7:37); the tax-collector (19:2); women (8:2); and children (18:17).
- Jesus refers often to: praise to God the Father (7:16); Christ's prayer life (6:12); the Holy Spirit (1:35); giving to God's work (6:38); bearing spiritual fruit (6:43); handling

finances wisely (16:1); true discipleship (9:23); and the kingdom of God (6:20).
- Jesus calls Himself the Son of Man—equal with the Father in His divine attributes, but a humble, caring man in His humanity.
- Luke carefully follows Jesus' ministry from His home town of Nazareth to His crucifixion in Jerusalem, and the divine mandate that led Him (9:22).
- Jesus' message was that He came to earth "to seek and to save that which was lost" (19:10).

Here are a few suggestions for using *Good News for the Family* effectively in your family devotions that were listed in the first book of this series *Growing a Wise Family – 100 Devotionals from the Book of Proverbs*:

1. Approach each devotional with great anticipation, desiring to enjoy each other as you discover the practical truths of the Word. If profitable questions or discussions come up as you progress through a devotional, then stop and spend appropriate time there. You can always start at that same point in the devotional the next day.
2. It's probably best for a parent to read the devotionals aloud rather than your children, so that dad or mom can direct the discussion. If possible, prepare by reading each devotional yourself prior to your family time.
3. There are three questions following each devotional that usually increase in difficulty from one through three. The answers provided are only a resource. Feel free to answer as you prefer.
4. Several questions ask for your child's personal opinion on a matter. You might want to ask each child the same question. Their answers may surprise and inspire you with ideas for further discussion.
5. At the bottom of many of the devotionals you will see references to the other gospel books. This "harmony of the gospels" refers to passages written by Matthew, Mark, and John about the same incident covered in that particular Luke devotional. These passages often add details not found in Luke.

6. If possible, pray before your family meets for the devotional time, that the children will be taught and God will be glorified.

Luke's emphasis in his gospel was to constantly point to the person and attributes of Jesus Christ. In order to fully capture the spirit of this gospel, I urge you to maintain that same emphasis.

# TABLE OF CONTENTS

1. Who Is Your Family Historian?
2. Opening For The Main Event
3. Does God Spoil Our Plans?
4. Don't Be Afraid!
5. What If The Pharisees Planned It?
6. A Man Named Simeon
7. Was Jesus Really Lost?
8. Growing Up In Galilee
9. Developing A Taste For Locusts
10. Snakes That Needed Baptizing
11. I'm Humble And Proud Of It
12. Four More Baptisms
13. Jesus Versus Satan In The Desert
14. A Prophet Without Profit
15. People With Itchy Ears
16. Putting Demons In Their Place
17. A Good Day's Fishing
18. The Leper Who Trusted Jesus
19. Jesus' Invitation—"Follow Me!"
20. Ouch! I Think I Need A Doctor
21. Is "More" Prayer Always Better?
22. There's A Log In My Eye
23. An Apple Tree Always Grows Apples
24. The Best Foundation
25. The Soldier Who Loved His Servant
26. What Amazes You?
27. Do We Look For Someone Else?
28. The Sweet Aroma Of Repentance
29. Forgiven Much And Little
30. The Power Of Trust
31. Sleeping Through The Storm
32. Faith In God Is Always Right
33. Little Is Much, When God Is In It
34. When Losing Our Life Means Finding It
35. Who Is The Greatest? Who's Number One?
36. I Want To Follow You, Lord; But First.....
37. Who In The World Is My Neighbor?
38. It Takes A Samaritan

39. Martha Was Anxious And Angry
40. Only One Thing Is Important
41. When In Doubt, Keep On Praying!
42. What Is The Sign Of Jonah?
43. The Eye—A Two-Way Street
44. Who Wants A Dirty Cup?
45. Who Are You Calling A Hypocrite?
46. How Much Are You Worth?
47. Is God Fair?
48. God Promises To Provide For Us
49. He Set His Face To Go To Jerusalem
50. Why All People Don't Get Saved—Choice
51. Why All People Don't Get Saved—Pride
52. Why All People Don't Get Saved—Stubbornness
53. Where Are You Sitting At The Table?
54. Should We Hate Our Own Family?
55. When A Plan Comes Together
56. Salt Is Good—At Times
57. "Until" Is Different Than "If."
58. Celebrate With Me!
59. What Does It Mean To Be A "Son" Or "Daughter"?
60. It's All About Me
61. What's A Steward And What Does She Do?
62. Making The Wrong Choice
63. Lazarus And The Rich Man
64. What Hell Is Like
65. How Many Times Do I Have To Forgive?
66. A Thanker, An Ignorer, Or A Whiner
67. When Jesus Comes In Glory
68. Just Too Full Of Alabama
69. Faith To Pray
70. Faith For Salvation
71. Faith For God's Fellowship
72. Faith To Trust What God Says
73. God Constantly Seeks The Lost
74. Jesus' Grand Entrance Into Jerusalem
75. When Even The Rocks Sing
76. The Day Jesus Cried
77. Countdown To Calvary
78. Who's Your Boss?

79. The Human Brain Versus The Computer
80. Where Does Courage Come From?
81. Giving All You've Got
82. When Jesus Returns A Second Time
83. With Privilege Comes Responsibility
84. Jesus' Last Passover With His Disciples
85. The Initiation Of The Lord's Supper
86. I'm The Greatest! Or Am I?
87. The Garden Of Sadness And Sleep
88. Betrayed With A Kiss
89. When The Big Fisherman Cried
90. Jesus Prays For His Persecutors
91. The Promise Of Paradise
92. "Behold Your Mother!"
93. Why Did God The Father Forsake His Son?
94. The Bitter Drink
95. "It Is Finished!"
96. When They Forgot To Remember
97. The Bible Is "His-story"
98. A Roller Coaster Of Emotions
99. "Proclaimers" To The Whole World
100. When Jesus Returned To Heaven

*Family historian*

## 1. WHO IS YOUR FAMILY HISTORIAN?

*Inasmuch as many have undertaken to compile [write] an account of the things accomplished [that happened] among us ... it seemed fitting [right] for me as well, having investigated everything carefully from the beginning, to write it out for you ...*
*Luke 1:1, 3*

Every family needs a historian! How I wish I had written down the actual historical facts of my family while my parents were still alive. I believe both sets of my grandparents came from England—but where exactly? I know nothing about my grandparents on my father's side, other than that they owned a farm north of Toronto, Canada. I could have gotten so many details from my dad, but I never thought of it.

I wish too that I had been our own family historian, keeping track of dates and details on what our family did. It would be so much fun to look back now on our "story" and remember the fun times we had together.

A Gentile (non-Jew) doctor named Luke was a historian around two thousand years ago. God used him to write one of the books of the Bible, the third of four books called the Gospels. Luke was a friend and traveling companion of the apostle Paul. Since both men became Christians after Jesus rose from the dead and returned to heaven, Dr. Luke had to get his facts on the Savior's life from interviewing people. If you've ever been to the doctor, you realize that they know how to ask the right questions to get accurate information.

Luke's goal was to investigate carefully all the details of Jesus' life from just before His birth until His return to heaven. He then wrote the details up in the form of a letter to a friend named Theophilus.

Well, how about it? Is there anyone in your family interested in being the family historian? Who knows—maybe you could even use the story of your family to write a best selling book!

## WHAT DO YOU THINK?

1. Who was Luke, what did he do for a living, who did he travel with, and who did he write this letter to?

2. Since Luke was not a disciple of Christ when the Savior was on earth, how did he get such accurate details of the Lord's life and death?

3. Are you interested in being your family historian?

## ANSWERS TO YOUR QUESTIONS

1. *Luke was a Gentile or non-Jew who was a doctor. He traveled with the apostle Paul when Paul went on his missionary journeys. Dr. Luke wrote his "gospel" to a friend named Theophilus, but he also wrote it to us.*

2. *Luke interviewed a lot of people to get the facts. Being a doctor, he knew how to ask the right questions. The gospel of Luke has a lot more details about people and events than the other three, Matthew, Mark, and John.*

3. *Personal opinion. You might want to ask each child.*

## 2. OPENING FOR THE MAIN EVENT

*And he will turn back many of the sons of Israel to the Lord their God. And it is he who will go as a forerunner before Him in the spirit and power of Elijah... so as to make ready a people prepared for the Lord.*
*Luke 1:16, 17*

Have you noticed that before certain "big name" events, there will often be a lesser known person or group who will "open" and prepare the audience? Their main job is not so much to draw attention to themselves as to prepare the audience for the famous act to follow.

Some TV shows will have a comedian or musician prepare the studio audience for the "star" before the program actually starts. Music groups will have an unknown band open their concert—to get the audience in the right mood for the main attraction.

God did something like that before the arrival of His beloved Son here on earth. We read here in Luke that Zacharias the priest and his wife Elizabeth were given a special gift from God in their old age—a son whose name was to be John. When John grew up, his full-time job was to announce the arrival on earth of Jesus Christ to the people of Israel—to prepare the way ahead of the Savior's birth.

John's birth was certainly a miracle, but another miracle occurred over 790 years before he was born. The Jewish prophet Isaiah predicted that God would not only send His Son to earth, but that someone else would "open" or "prepare the way" for Him. Isaiah said, "A voice is calling, 'Clear the way for the Lord in the wilderness; make smooth in the desert a highway for our God'" (Isaiah 40:3).

And sure enough, John was that man—he fulfilled Isaiah's prophecy. How do we fit in to this? Our responsibility as Christians is to tell the world that Jesus already came, He died to pay for our sins, and He is coming again one day. In a sense, we are also "opening" for Him.

## WHAT DO YOU THINK?

1. What did Isaiah the prophet predict would happen one day in the future?

2. This man whose name was John was born into the world in a miraculous way. What was that?

3. In what way was John to tell the nation of Israel to get ready for the coming of the Lord or Messiah?

## ANSWERS TO YOUR QUESTIONS

1. *Isaiah predicted or prophesied that God would one day raise up a person who would live in the wilderness and whose message to Israel would be that they should prepare themselves for the coming of "the Lord" or God's Son.*

2. *John's parents, Zacharias and Elizabeth, were quite old when he was born. His mother was what was called "barren" or unable to have children. Zacharias had trouble believing the angel Gabriel when he announced to him that he and his wife were going to be parents of a special son.*

3. *They were to prepare their hearts to believe on the Lord Jesus when He came. The main way that Israel could prepare for Him would be to admit that they were lost sinners without any hope of eternal life in themselves, and to repent of their sin.*

*Mary's surprise visitor*

## 3. DOES GOD SPOIL OUR PLANS?

*Now in the sixth month the angel Gabriel was sent from God to a city in Galilee, called Nazareth, to a virgin engaged to a man whose name was Joseph, of the descendants [relatives] of David; and the virgin's name was Mary ... And Mary said, "Behold, the bondslave of the Lord; be it done to me according to Your word."*
*Luke 1: 26, 27, 38*

I'm sure God thought very carefully about who He would choose to give birth to Jesus on earth. There was no woman in all of Israel who was perfect, but there must have been certain things about Mary that pleased Him. Here are some possibilities:

- Mary had kept herself morally pure (verse 27).
- She was humble—she called herself "the servant of the Lord" (verse 38).
- Mary wanted to obey God's Word, even though she couldn't imagine herself giving birth to the Messiah of Israel.
- She trusted in God as her Savior. She joyfully said, "My spirit rejoices in God my Savior" (verse 47).

Mary was most likely in her late teens when she was engaged to Joseph. Like most young girls she probably had her wedding all planned out in her mind—what dress she would wear, who would be invited to the ceremony, even where she and Joseph would live once they were married.

And then the angel Gabriel appeared to Mary. What a shock that would be! But what the angel shared with her was even more shocking. Through a miracle, she was going to give birth to God's Son here on earth so that He could be the Savior of the world and the eternal King of Israel.

Wow! Can you imagine a young teenage girl trying to get her mind around that? There go her plans for a wedding! And the special dress! How does she explain being pregnant to her friends and family? Can't you just hear them? "You talked with which angel? Who's the father of the baby?"

You can't help but respect Mary when you read her response to the angel: "Be it done to me according to your word" (verse 37). Have you noticed that God's plans turn out to be better than our own?

## WHAT DO YOU THINK?

1. Where did Mary and Joseph live when they were engaged? Can you find their town on a map of Israel?

2. After Mary got over the shock of the angel's announcement, what was her response?

3. Although we don't know for sure, what are some possible reasons God chose Mary to give birth to God's beloved Son Jesus?

## ANSWERS TO YOUR QUESTIONS

*1. Mary and Joseph lived in a small town called Nazareth, about 20 miles west of the Sea of Galilee.*

*2. Once the angel Gabriel explained who she would give birth to and how it would take place, Mary humbly said she was the servant (slave) of God. She willingly accepted whatever God's will was for her.*

*3. Mary was morally pure. She had a good reputation. She was humble and called herself "the servant of the Lord." She was willing to obey God even though it was almost impossible to imagine—giving birth to Israel's Messiah without a husband. It seems that Mary had already trusted in God as her Savior.*

*No need for fear*

## 4. DON'T BE AFRAID!

*And the angel said to her, "Do not be afraid, Mary; for you have found favor with God."*
*Luke 1:30*

Have you ever been scared silly? When I was around ten years of age, I was so frightened one day I can still feel the fear just thinking about it. It was a summer afternoon and I took a nap. When I woke up, my parents and sister were not in the house. Why didn't they wake me up before they left? Where would they go without me?

I went into the bathroom and all of a sudden I heard blaring music. It seemed to be outside the house and inside too. My first thought was that Jesus had come back to earth to take all believers to heaven (the Rapture). Maybe my family had gone up to meet Jesus in the air—and I had been left behind. I've heard people say that they were so frightened their heart stopped. Not me! Mine was racing a hundred miles an hour. Where was the music coming from?

I looked out the bathroom window just in time to see a car drive around the corner with a large bell speaker on top advertising some event. I don't have to tell you how relieved I was. When my folks got home from their walk, I kept them in my sight for quite a while.

God is so understanding of how easily we get frightened. When the angel Gabriel appeared to John's father, Zacharias, and later on to Mary, he comforted them with, "Do not be afraid." Even when announcing Jesus' coming birth, the angel of the Lord assured Joseph "…do not be afraid to take Mary as your wife…" (Matthew 1:20).

There are many examples throughout the Bible where the Lord or one of His angels unexpectedly appeared to people. Remember when the disciples were in a boat during a vicious storm and suddenly Jesus approached them walking on the water? We read, "And when the disciples saw Him walking on the sea, they were frightened, saying, 'It is a ghost!' And they cried out for fear. But immediately Jesus spoke to them, saying, 'Take courage, it is I; do not be afraid" (Matthew 14:26, 27). Isn't the Lord Jesus wonderful how He even wants to calm our fears?

# WHAT DO YOU THINK?

1. Can you remember a time when you were so frightened that the details of the incident are still clear in your memory?

2. When God appeared suddenly to people throughout the Bible, His first words were often, "Don't be afraid!" What does that show us about His personality?

3. Look up Isaiah 41:10 and explain it in your own words.

# ANSWERS TO YOUR QUESTIONS

1. *Personal opinion.*

2. *It shows us that He knows we are easily frightened. He wants to comfort us and keep us from unnecessary stress and harm.*

3. *Personal opinion.*

*If Pharisees were in charge*

## 5. WHAT IF THE PHARISEES PLANNED IT?

*And Joseph also went up from Galilee, from the city of Nazareth, to Judea, to the city of David, which is called Bethlehem …… in order to register, along with Mary, who was engaged to him, and was with child.*
Luke 2:4, 5

We know that God was in charge of every detail of our Savior's birth, but can you imagine how different it would have been if the Pharisees would have planned it? Below are some thoughts about that. [NOTE: The Pharisees were a popular religious group in Israel during Jesus' day. They believed they were God's special treasure and refused to associate with the heathen (Gentiles). They believed in angels, spirits, and the resurrection. They also prided themselves on knowing the Old Testament. The Pharisees added a lot of their own rules to God's laws that had to do with the "outside" i.e. hand washing, and ignored their sinful heart attitudes "inside." They hated Jesus!]

- God chose unknown peasants, Joseph and Mary, to be Jesus' parents. The Pharisees would no doubt have chosen a wealthy couple, most likely from a long line of well-to-do Pharisees.
- God chose a couple from the backwater town of Nazareth (Luke 2:4, 5). Because family name was so important to them, the Pharisees would probably have chosen people who had high status in the social register, probably a couple from Jerusalem.
- God's plan was for Jesus to be born during a census, when the people were scattered, having traveled to their home towns for a "head count" (2:1). For the Pharisees, a huge audience would have been a must, so they would have chosen a time and place where large crowds were gathered—for them the time of the Jewish Passover in Jerusalem would have been ideal.
- When it was almost time for Mary to have her baby, she traveled about eighty miles on a donkey! Would the Pharisees have planned that, as God did? Never! If they had been in charge when Mary's family members first heard that she was

expecting, she would have been put under the care of a good doctor…in Jerusalem, of course!
- We know that God's choice for a birthplace for His Son was an inn in Bethlehem, one that was already full. That drafty, smelly barn would be at the absolute bottom of the Pharisees' list; only a 5-star hotel in Jerusalem would serve for the new family—close to the doctor who would assist the delivery.
- God chose His Son's birth to be announced to shepherds by angels. Do you think that's how the Pharisees would have done it? No! It would definitely have been the chief priest of the Jewish temple who would have heard the news first. And he would have been perfectly capable of announcing the blessed event to the large crowds—no need of angels! (2:8-10).

Yes, if the Pharisees of Jesus' day were in charge of the arrival of God's Son on earth, it might have been something glitzy like the Super Bowl. But God planned that a poor couple from a small town would travel almost a hundred miles to give birth to the Savior of the world in a dirty barn. And how would He first announce that birth? Angels from heaven would appear to simple shepherds in a field.

God's ways and His plans are so much better than anything that the Pharisees (or any of us) could ever devise.

## WHAT DO YOU THINK?

1. If the Pharisees had been in charge of Jesus' birth, what location would they most likely have chosen for the blessed event?

2. Rather than simple shepherds being the first to announce the Messiah's birth, who would most likely have had that privilege?

3. Why do you think God chose to plan out Jesus' arrival on earth the way He did?

## ANSWERS TO YOUR QUESTIONS

*1. The Pharisees would likely have chosen Jerusalem which was the city of greatest importance in all of Israel, and where the greatest crowds were.*

*2. Again, if the Pharisees were planning all the details of the Messiah's entrance on earth, the high priest would most likely have been the one out front making all the important announcements. (I wonder if they had press conferences in those days.)*

*3. It's impossible to know God's mind, but as you read the New Testament you see time after time how He chose the simple and humble way, rather than the big, splashy, expensive way. It shows that God is for every man, woman, and child—both rich and poor.*

## 6. A MAN NAMED SIMEON

*And behold, there was a man in Jerusalem whose name was Simeon; and this man was righteous and devout [worshipful], looking for the consolation of Israel [the coming of Israel's deliverer]; and the Holy Spirit was upon him. And it had been revealed to him by the Holy Spirit that he would not see death before he had seen the Lord's Christ. And he came in the Spirit into the temple; and when the parents brought in the child Jesus, to carry out for Him the custom of the Law, then he took Him into his arms, and blessed God...*
*Luke 2:25-28*

Simeon was an unusual man. First, he was one of a small group of Jews during the time that Jesus was born on earth, who loved and obeyed God. Because he believed the Old Testament Scriptures, he believed Isaiah's prophecy: "For a child will be born to us, a son will be given to us; and the government will rest on His shoulders; and His name will be called Wonderful Counselor, Mighty God, Eternal Father, Prince of Peace" (Isaiah 9:6).

Simeon was also unusual because God the Holy Spirit informed him personally that he would see the long-awaited Messiah, the Savior of the world, before he died.

Can you imagine his joy when he walked into the temple and there was God's beloved Son, Jesus, in his earthly parents' arms? I'm sure Jesus didn't look much like the Creator of the universe right then—more like a helpless baby. But Simeon knew who He was and he immediately took the baby in his arms.

Soon after God created Adam and Eve, and while they were still in the Garden of Eden, He promised that He would provide a Savior to pay the sin debt of all mankind (Genesis 3:15). Thousands of years later, we hear the angels announcing to the shepherds, "...for behold, I bring you good news of great joy which shall be for all the people..." (Luke 2:10). That good news was the birth of Jesus, the Messiah.

As Simeon held the Son of God in his arms, he prophesied that some men would love Him while others would hate Him. He even predicted that Jesus' earthly mother Mary would experience great sadness—when Jesus suffered and died on Calvary's cross.

Now that Simeon had seen Jesus, he was ready to pass from this life into the presence of God the Father.

## WHAT DO YOU THINK?

1. What did Simeon want to experience more than anything, before he died?

2. How did Simeon know that he would see the Messiah in person on this earth?

3. What did Simeon mean when he prophesied to Mary, "...and a sword will pierce even your own soul..." (Luke 2:35).

## ANSWERS TO YOUR QUESTIONS

1. *Luke writes that Simeon was "looking for the consolation of Israel"—in other words, the deliverer, the Messiah, God the Father's only Son, the Savior of the world.*

2. *God the Holy Spirit revealed it to Simeon that he would see the Messiah of Israel before he died.*

3. *He meant that Mary would experience a crushing sadness at some point in her life. Since she was there when Jesus was nailed to the cross (see John 19:26), and she saw his pain and agony, this is probably the event to which Simeon was referring.*

## 7. WAS JESUS REALLY LOST?

*And His parents used to go to Jerusalem every year at the Feast of the Passover. And when He became twelve, they went up there according to the custom of the Feast; and as they were returning ... the boy Jesus stayed behind in Jerusalem.*
*Luke 2:41-43*

When our daughter Kelley was about four years old, her mom and I took her with us to a department store. I had gone up to the second floor and was on my way down the escalator. I spotted Del and Kelley just as Del moved around a rack of dresses and out of our daughter's sight. For that brief moment Kelley was alone with no parent in sight. I will never forget the look of panic on her face as she realized, "I'm alone in a strange place and I can't see my mommy or daddy." How thrilled she was when Del came into sight again!

Today's verses tell us about a time when Jesus was twelve years old, and He visited Jerusalem with His parents at Passover time. When the family began the trip back to Nazareth, Jesus stayed behind in the temple without Mary and Joseph knowing it. They finally found Him, three days later, in deep discussion with the temple teachers.

Why do you suppose Jesus, the perfect Son of God, would do that? The Bible only gives us the briefest of clues. When Mary asked Him, "Son, why have you treated us this way?" Jesus made it plain that He was first of all the Son of Almighty God. His answer was respectful but clear, "Why is it that you were looking for Me? Did you not know that I had to be in My Father's house" (Luke 2:49)? In other words, He was saying, "Before anything else—even your wishes—I'm responsible to listen for and obey God the Father's words."

This is not the answer of a rebellious soon-to-be teenager. Verse 51 tells us that Jesus "continued in subjection to them." During His brief time on earth, Joseph and Mary were His earthly parents, but He always was and always will be God the Son—the exact image of His heavenly Father (Hebrews 1:3).

# WHAT DO YOU THINK?

1. Can you think of a time when you felt like you were lost? Do you remember what thoughts and feelings you had?

2. Why were Joseph, Mary, and Jesus in Jerusalem in the first place?

3. When Mary rebuked Jesus for not staying with them, what did Jesus say in response?

# ANSWERS TO YOUR QUESTIONS

1. *Personal opinion. You may want to ask each child.*

2. *They traveled from their home town of Nazareth to Jerusalem to observe the Jewish feast called the Passover.*

3. *Jesus asked them why they were looking for Him. Then He reminded them that He first of all had to obey His heavenly Father's will. He was their earthly son, but He was primarily the Son of God.*

*Jesus, a maturing young man*

## 8. GROWING UP IN GALILEE

*And Jesus kept increasing in wisdom and stature [height], and in favor with God and men.*
*Luke 2:52*

I've often wondered what Jesus' growing up years in Nazareth were like—as a teenager and young man in His twenties. On the one hand He was always God the Son, and yet in His time on earth, His appearance was like that of any other Galilean. Was He taller, stronger, and more handsome than His neighbors? As God, He could have chosen any appearance He wanted. The prophet Isaiah wrote, "…He has no stately form or majesty that we should look upon Him, nor appearance that we should be attracted to Him" (Isaiah 53:2).

So it seems like it was decided in heaven before Jesus' birth that He would not rely on His good looks (like David), His strength (like Samson), or His height (like Saul), in order to draw people.

But for the first thirty years of His life on earth—prior to beginning His ministry—He must have been a model son to Joseph and Mary. He wouldn't have gotten into selfish arguments with His brothers and sisters; He wouldn't have started fights with the local bully; and He definitely wouldn't have stolen grapes from the vineyard down the street.

There are so few details in the Bible about those years. We know He worked with Joseph as a carpenter (Mark 6:3). To His neighbors and relatives Jesus must have seemed like any other young man growing up in Nazareth except for one thing—He never committed a single sin.

Today's verse explains that although He was the perfect Son of God, He still had a human mind and body. So, He developed or matured like any other young man His age. Luke tells us that He grew mentally (in wisdom), physically (in stature), spiritually (in favor with God), and socially (in favor with man).

Wouldn't it have been great to have been Jesus' next door neighbor during those years?

## WHAT DO YOU THINK?

1. When Jesus was growing up, was there anything about His appearance that would cause you to notice Him in a crowd of young men?

2. What kept Jesus from getting into trouble like some other boys His age?

3. If Jesus was still the perfect Son of God during His thirty-three years on earth, how could He grow mentally, physically, spiritually, and socially?

## ANSWERS TO YOUR QUESTIONS

*1. God planned it that His beloved Son Jesus would not attract people by His physical appearance, during His time on earth. It was His kind, loving nature and the fact that He always spoke the truth that drew people to Jesus.*

*2. Although Jesus looked like most other young men His age, He was still the holy Son of God—Creator of the entire universe. As God, He never sinned and never will.*

*3. When Jesus came into the world as a baby, He never stopped being God the Son. The divine or God-part of His nature could not grow and mature because He was already perfect—the exact image of God the Father. However, His human body and mind would develop like that of any other male, and He would learn and grow through the things He experienced.*

*Repentance*

## 9. DEVELOPING A TASTE FOR LOCUSTS

*And he [John] came into all the district around the Jordan, preaching a baptism of repentance for the forgiveness of sins.*
*Luke 3:3*

John the Baptist would certainly stand out in a crowd—even in his day. He wore clothes made out of camel hair and his meals were mostly locusts (a cousin of the grasshopper) and wild honey. There probably wasn't much else to eat out in the desert.

John must have been a powerful preacher despite how he looked, because Matthew writes, "Then Jerusalem was going out to him, and all Judea, and all the district around the Jordan; and they were being baptized by him in the Jordan River, as they confessed their sins" (Matthew 3:5, 6).

What was John's message that caused crowds of people to go out in the wilderness and be baptized by him? It helps to remember that John was preparing the way for Jesus, the Messiah, who had not yet started His ministry. John preached that people should *repent* of their sin because the kingdom of heaven was soon to arrive in the person of Jesus.

The word "repent" is not heard very much these days, but its meaning is very important. Have you ever planned to go outside to do something with your friends? When you look out the window you see it's raining very hard and there's mud everywhere. You change your mind and attitude about being outside—you decide that being warm and dry is a better choice. Doing that, in biblical terms, is repenting.

God the Holy Spirit was working through John to prepare the Jewish people for Christ's message of salvation. Before they could receive Christ as their Savior, they needed to realize that they were sinners who needed saving. Their hearts were hard and self-confident—certainly not soft and open to the teaching of God's own Son, Jesus.

As John preached to the Jewish people who came out of the cities of Judea to hear him, some had a serious change of mind and attitude. They realized that their lives were full of sinful thoughts and actions, and deserved God's judgment—they repented. Other people continued to have hard hearts and probably mocked John and his message.

We still see people making those same two choices today.

[See also: Matthew 3:1-6; Mark 1:1-8)

## WHAT DO YOU THINK?

1. Where did John spend most of his adult life, what did he wear, and what did he mainly eat?

2. What was John's main focus in life and what message did he preach?

3. What does *repentance* or *to repent* mean?

## ANSWERS TO YOUR QUESTIONS

1. *John spent most of his adult life in the wilderness around the Jordan River. He wore clothes made from camel hair, and mostly ate locusts and wild honey.*

2. *John's main focus in life was to prepare the way for Jesus Christ and to prepare the Jewish people around Jerusalem for Jesus' message of salvation.*

3. *To repent means to change your mind and attitude about something. To repent of your sin means to change your mind and attitude about that sin, which generally leads to confessing it to God. You might stubbornly hold onto your sin and even make excuses. But when you repent of it, you admit to yourself and God that you were wrong and you want God's forgiveness.*

*John's baptism*

## 10. SNAKES THAT NEEDED BAPTIZING

*He therefore began saying to the multitudes who were going out to be baptized by him, "You brood of vipers [snakes], who warned you to flee from the wrath to come?"*
*Luke 3:7*

    Why do you suppose John called the people *snakes* who came out to the Jordan River to hear him and be baptized? He was not kidding himself into thinking that every individual in the crowds that were flocking to him wanted to confess his sin and learn about the Messiah. Some were probably just wanting to see this strange "desert creature" out of curiosity. Others, like the Pharisees and elders, wanted to put an end to any competition before it got too popular. John diagnosed the situation correctly. There were plenty of *snakes-in-the-grass,* and he planned to expose them.

    As the Jews who lived in and around Jerusalem came to John, they heard him telling about Jesus Christ the Messiah who would soon be coming, and He would provide the only way of salvation. In order for these Jewish people to receive Jesus' message, they first had to understand that they were lost in their sin and headed for hell. John taught them that they needed to confess their sin to God and then be baptized by him in the Jordan River.

    Did this baptism save these people? No, in no way! It simply prepared them for when Jesus began to teach that belief or trust in Him was the only way to become His child forever.

    How about you and me? Should we undergo a "baptism of repentance" like the people of John's day? No. Certainly not! Jesus came and died on the cross to pay for our sin. John's baptism was only for a short period of time and was intended to "prepare the way" for Jesus. His baptism looked *ahead* a few weeks or months to the arrival of Jesus—the carpenter from Nazareth and the Son of God.

    Today, when people realize that they cannot save themselves and trust in Jesus' death, burial, and resurrection (see I Corinthians 15:1-5), they are born again. As a testimony to the world and as a step of faith in obedience to God's Word, a new Christian will be baptized. This baptism looks *back* to three days in history on a hill outside Jerusalem when Christ's dear body was nailed to a wooden cross and pierced with a Roman soldier's spear.

The book of Acts explains this difference well: "And Paul said, 'John baptized with the baptism of repentance, telling the people to believe in Him who was coming after him, that is in Jesus.' And when they heard this, they were baptized in the name of the Lord Jesus" (Acts 19:4, 5).

[See also: Matthew 3:7-10]

## WHAT DO YOU THINK?

1. Who was John the Baptist calling "vipers" or snakes?

2. What did John's baptism mean to the Jewish people who came out to the Jordan area to hear him?

3. How would you explain the difference between John's baptism and the Christian's baptism of today?

## ANSWERS TO YOUR QUESTIONS

1. *John was speaking to the Jewish people who lived in and around Jerusalem and who came out to the area of the Jordan River to hear him. They were proud because they were "sons of Abraham" and didn't admit that they were lost sinners.*

2. *John's baptism was for those who repented or admitted that they were sinners. It was an outward demonstration that they had confessed their sin and were ready to hear the Savior who would soon be there.*

3. *John's baptism of repentance looked "ahead" to the coming Messiah, Jesus Christ. Christian baptism today looks "back" to Christ's death on the cross where He paid for the sins of the whole world with His blood.*

*Humility and pride*

## 11. I'M HUMBLE AND PROUD OF IT

*"...and do not begin to say to yourselves, 'We have Abraham for our father'...as for me, I baptize you with water; but One is coming who is mightier than I, and I am not fit to untie the thong of His sandals."*

*Luke 3:8, 16*

After a medical appointment the other day, I began to talk with the technician about Jesus Christ and where he stood as far as salvation. His response was almost identical to that of so many other people I've talked with. He believes he is a "good person"—good enough, at least, to be allowed into heaven.

There are at least three things wrong with that thinking:
- Christ died for *sinners,* not "good people." Since we are all lost sinners, from God's point of view, no person is good enough to deserve heaven. If good people were allowed into heaven, then Christ never would have had to come to earth and die on Calvary to pay our sin-debt.
- There are a lot of jokes about the apostle Peter being the guard at the "pearly gates of heaven." In most of the stories, it's Peter who decides who enters on the basis of how good they've been. The problem is that this is not what the Bible teaches (Romans 5:8, 9). Only people who admit they are sinners and believe in Christ's sacrifice for them, are allowed in—only *forgiven* people.
- If you believe you are good enough for heaven, how good is "enough?" When you ask unsaved people this question, they will often say something like, "Well, I think I'm OK. I may have lied, cheated, or stolen (just little things), but I have never committed a crime." James 2:10 says, "For whoever keeps the whole law and yet stumbles in one point, he has become guilty of all."

What is that verse saying? Since everyone who ever lived has committed at least one sin, we are all guilty of breaking every single law of God.

Our *pride* says, "I'm good enough to deserve heaven," while *humility* says, "I am a lost sinner and I need God's free gift of salvation." Where do you stand?

[See also: Matthew 3:11, 12; Mark 1:7, 8]

## WHAT DO YOU THINK?

1. What answer can you usually expect when you ask a stranger, "On what are you depending to get to heaven when you die?"

2. What kind of person did Christ die for? What kind of person will go to heaven?

3. According to James 2:10, what happens if you commit even one sin in your lifetime? Besides Jesus, has there ever been a perfect person live on earth?

## ANSWERS TO YOUR QUESTIONS

1. *Very often, if a person is an unbeliever, they will answer your question about heaven with a statement something like, "I think I'm good enough to go to heaven when I die."*

2. *Jesus Christ died on the cross for lost sinners. People who are forgiven by God because they trusted in Christ's death, burial, and resurrection, will go to heaven.*

3. *James 2:10 says that if you commit even one sin, you are guilty of breaking every single law of God. Only Jesus lived a perfect life on earth, because He is God and man.*

*Five different baptisms*

## 12. FOUR MORE BAPTISMS

*Now it came about when all the people were baptized, that Jesus also was baptized, and while He was praying, heaven was opened, and the Holy Spirit descended upon Him in bodily form like a dove, and a voice came out of heaven, "[You] are My beloved Son, in [You] I am well-pleased."*
*Luke 3:21, 22*

In Devotional ten, we read about John's baptism of repentance in the Jordan River. His message was that the Jews should change their minds and attitudes about their sin, in preparation for Jesus' coming. John baptized those who did repent. Luke 3:16 tells us, "...He [Christ] will baptize you with the Holy Spirit and fire." Luke is talking here to two groups of people—those who receive Christ by faith will be baptized by the Holy Spirit. In other words, at the time they believe the Gospel, the Holy Spirit will come to live inside them (1 Corinthians 12:13). The other group are those who want nothing to do with Jesus—like the Pharisees. They will be "baptized by fire" or be judged by God and sent to hell for all eternity.

The fourth kind of baptism in the New Testament is *believers' baptism*. When a person puts her trust in Jesus' death, burial, and resurrection as payment for her sins, she becomes a child of God forever. The next step for this new Christian is to be baptized in actual water as a testimony to all that she is a believer who now belongs to Christ. We will talk more about this later.

The last type of baptism refers to the time when Jesus Himself was baptized by John. This was a unique time that only happened once and could never happen to anyone else. Jesus was about thirty years of age and had been living in Nazareth.

One day while John was preaching by the Jordan, Jesus suddenly appeared and asked John to baptize Him. This was the beginning of Christ's ministry here on earth. His only explanation to a bewildered John was that it was necessary "to fulfill all righteousness." This probably means that it was God the Father's will.

The word "baptism" doesn't have to be confusing. Since John's "baptism of repentance" and Jesus' baptism "to fulfill all righteousness" no longer apply to us today, we just have three other occasions of this word:
- The baptism of "judgment by fire" where Jesus will judge unbelievers by fire (Luke 3:16).
- The baptism or entering of the Holy Spirit into our bodies, the moment we trust in Jesus (1 Corinthians 12:13).
- The baptism of the believer in actual water following our salvation (Acts 8:36).

[See also Matthew 3:13-17; Mark 1:9-11; John 1:29-34]

## WHAT DO YOU THINK?

1. How did John's "baptism of repentance" differ from the "believers' baptism"?

2. What did John mean when he said, "He [Jesus] will baptize you with the Holy Spirit and fire"?

3. Why won't Jesus' baptism ever be repeated by anyone else?

## ANSWERS TO YOUR QUESTIONS

1. *John's message was that the Jews should change their minds and attitudes about their sin, in preparation for Jesus' coming. John baptized those who did repent. When a person believes the Gospel and is born again, they are a Christian. One of the first steps of obedience a new believer should consider is to be baptized in water. This is a testimony to all present, that the one baptized now belongs to Christ.*

2. *Jesus was talking to two groups of people. He promised that the Holy Spirit would place all believers into the Christian family, and would literally enter their bodies. Those who reject Christ's free gift will one day face God's judgment by fire.*

3. *Jesus was baptized at the beginning of His ministry, to follow His Father's will. The Holy Spirit descended upon Jesus in the form of a dove, and God the Father spoke lovingly of His Son's obedience. This baptism of Jesus in actual water will never happen again.*

## 13. JESUS VERSUS SATAN IN THE DESERT

*And Jesus, full of the Holy Spirit, returned from the Jordan and was led about by the Spirit in the wilderness for forty days, being tempted by the devil.*
*Luke 4:1, 2*

Before Jesus even started His ministry of teaching and healing, God the Father allowed the Holy Spirit to lead Jesus into the desert to be tempted by the devil. Was it to prove to Satan right from the start that the Son of God was more powerful, in that He was God as well as man? Or was it mainly for Jesus' benefit, so that He could experience in person what we go through by being tempted daily?

Jesus took no food with Him so He went without eating for forty days. (If I go forty minutes past my meal time, I'm beginning to look for snacks.) The devil showed up when Jesus was at His weakest and tried to get Him to sin. The Son of God cannot sin because He is God. But He could certainly experience the anguish of being tempted to disobey God's Word.

Satan cuts to the chase right away and urges the Lord to turn stones into bread. What's wrong with that? It wasn't God the Father telling Jesus to do that, so He would have been obeying the devil. The Evil One tempts us too so we think we just have to have certain things, whether the Father wants us to or not.

Next, Satan suggests that if Jesus would worship him, he would give God's Son all the authority in the world. First of all, he only ruled the world as much as God allowed him to (John 12:31; John 14:30). Secondly, the Father already said that His Holy Son would rule all of the earth (Psalm 2:8). But first, Jesus had to die on the cross to pay for our sins, and Satan didn't want that.

Satan's final temptation was that Jesus leap off a high tower—probably in Jerusalem—to amaze people, so they would realize He was the Messiah. This was not the Father's plan either.

In each of the three temptations, Jesus stood on the Word of God. Don't you think that it would be pretty safe for us to do the same thing?

[See also: Matthew 4:1-11; Mark 1:12, 13]

## WHAT DO YOU THINK?

1. Was it possible for Jesus to give in to Satan's temptations, and therefore sin? Why or why not?

2. What are two possible reasons why Jesus went into the wilderness and allowed Satan to tempt Him?

3. What event had to take place before Christ would gloriously reign over all the kingdoms of the earth?

## ANSWERS TO YOUR QUESTIONS

1. *When Jesus was on earth, He was "the God-man," which means He was completely God, but also completely man. He set aside His glory to become man when He came into the world, but not His holiness as God.*

2. *The first possible reason was to remind Satan right from the beginning of His ministry on earth, that He was more powerful, even in His weakest physical condition. The other reason was possibly to experience Himself, the temptation that we face daily, for our encouragement (Hebrews 4:15).*

3. *Jesus had to die for the sins of the world on a Roman cross, before He would reign over the earth in all His glory.*

*Jesus returns to Nazareth*

## 14. A PROPHET WITHOUT PROFIT

*And He came to Nazareth, where He had been brought up; and as was His custom, He entered the synagogue on the Sabbath, and stood up to read. And the book of the prophet Isaiah was handed to Him.*
*Luke 4:16, 17*

Imagine standing up at school or work and announcing that you had just invented a capsule that could fly you to Mars and back in an hour. What would your audience think? They might just call for an ambulance!

A similar kind of situation took place one Saturday in Jesus' home town of Nazareth. It had been about one year since His baptism and He had been performing miracles in other towns (John 2-5). Everyone knew Him in the synagogue (local center of worship)—after all, they had seen Jesus grow up in the home of Joseph and Mary. Maybe Jesus had even built some furniture for them in Joseph's carpentry shop.

Jesus had probably stood up in their meetings before and read Old Testament verses. This time was different. He read the first verse of Isaiah 61 and part of verse two, and then He sat down. So far so good. But then He announced, "...Today this Scripture has been fulfilled in your hearing" (Luke 4:21).

What was so unusual about the verses He read? The prophet Isaiah, led by the Holy Spirit, was speaking about a coming Messiah—one sent by God to save the people of Israel physically (from their enemies), and spiritually (from their sins). Jesus was announcing that a new period of history was beginning, and He was the center or focal point. The long awaited Savior had finally come to Israel, and this neighbor of theirs claimed it was Him.

We have the privilege of looking back on history and knowing that these verses spoke only of Jesus. In fact, the whole Bible points to Him. This history is His-story!

[See also: Matthew 13:53-58; Mark 6:1-6]

## WHAT DO YOU THINK?

1. In today's lesson, Jesus was in His hometown. What town was it; what day of the week was it; and what building was he in?

2. What book of the Bible did Jesus read from?

3. In your own words, what did Jesus say when He finished reading, and why were the people so shocked?

## ANSWERS TO YOUR QUESTIONS

1. *Jesus was in Nazareth where He grew up. It was the Sabbath (Saturday), and He was in the synagogue (Jewish place of worship).*

2. *Jesus read from the book of Isaiah.*

3. *Jesus said, "Today this Scripture has been fulfilled in your hearing" (Luke 4:21). The people who heard Jesus knew that the verses He read applied to the coming Messiah and He was claiming that they spoke about Him.*

*Itching ears*

## 15. PEOPLE WITH ITCHY EARS

*And all were speaking well of Him, and wondering at the gracious words which were falling from His lips...And all in the synagogue were filled with rage as they heard these things; and they rose up and cast Him out of the city, and led Him to the brow of the hill...in order to throw Him down the cliff. But passing through their midst, He went His way.*
*Luke 4:22, 28-30*

What is wrong with these people? One minute they are praising Jesus for His wise and helpful words—the next minute they are like a crazed mob trying to kill Him. It's not as if Jesus was a stranger who wandered into town one day. He was their neighbor—they knew His whole family—He had walked the streets of Nazareth for thirty years.

What was it that angered the people so? Apparently Jesus had done some miracles earlier in the town of Capernaum, about twenty-five miles from Nazareth, and now they wanted Him to perform similar miracles in His hometown. He chose not to.

Jesus makes three truthful points with them:

- A prophet (or in this case, the Son of God) isn't welcomed or appreciated in His hometown where people know Him very well.
- Jesus didn't intend to heal every person in every city He visited. He always followed His Father's will while on earth, and only did what He was directed to do.
- Jesus reminded the Jewish people present that God also loves the Gentiles or non-Jews. The prophet Elijah healed a Gentile woman from Sidon, while Elisha healed Naaman the Syrian captain, also a Gentile.

There was a reason Jesus did not carry on a ministry of teaching and performing miracles in His hometown. They had no real interest in repenting of their sin and obeying God—they had *itchy* ears. The apostle Paul wrote to young Timothy, "...preach the word...For the time will come when they will not endure sound doctrine; but wanting to have their ears tickled, they will accumulate [hire] for themselves teachers in accordance [agreement] to their own [evil] desires" (2 Timothy 4:2, 3).

How sad for the people of Nazareth! Jesus most likely never returned to His home town.[1]

## WHAT DO YOU THINK?

1. What did the people of Nazareth want more than hearing and obeying Jesus' teaching?

2. What were two reasons that Jesus' listeners were angry enough to try and kill Him?

3. What does it mean in the Bible for people to have "itchy" ears?

## ANSWERS TO YOUR QUESTIONS

1. *The people of Nazareth wanted Jesus to perform miracles there like He had done earlier in Capernaum.*

2. *They were angry because:*
   - *Jesus was not doing miracles in their town like He had done elsewhere.*
   - *He reminded them that God healed those He chose to. At times He miraculously healed Gentiles and passed by Jews with similar diseases.*

3. *To have itchy ears means to want to have teachers who won't tell you what you need to hear, i.e. about your disobedience to God, but will tell you how great you are. It's like a dog that follows his master around so that he can get his ears scratched occasionally.*

*Evil spirits*

## 16. PUTTING DEMONS IN THEIR PLACE

*And demons also were coming out of many, crying out and saying, "You are the Son of God!" And rebuking them, He would not allow them to speak, because they knew Him to be the Christ.*
*Luke 4:41*

What was this particular Sabbath (Saturday) like for Jesus? The day begins in Capernaum where Jesus is teaching in the synagogue. There just happens to be a Jewish man there who has a demon (an evil spirit that follows Satan), living inside him. The evil spirit calls out, "Ha! What do we have to do with You, Jesus of Nazareth? Have You come to destroy us? I know who You are—the Holy One of God" (Luke 4:34)!

Jesus describes Satan well in John 8:44: "He was a murderer from the beginning, and does not stand in the truth, because there is no truth in him. Whenever he speaks a lie, he speaks from his own nature; for he is a liar, and the father of lies." I can imagine his evil demons are liars too. But confronted with God the Son, they could only tell the truth. So why wouldn't Jesus let them profess Him? Wouldn't that help convince the Jewish people that He was the King of the Jews?

Instead of that, we read, "And Jesus rebuked him, saying, 'Be quiet and come out of him'" (Luke 4:35)! It seems that Jesus did not want evil spirits to announce His coming to Israel—after all, they were *evil*. God had chosen John the Baptist to do that.

Following the meeting in the synagogue, Jesus went to the home of Simon Peter. Simon's wife's mother had a high fever and Jesus healed her in an instant, so that she was able to make lunch for them all. Jesus had power over evil spirits and over diseases of the body.

When the local people realized what Jesus was doing, they began to bring their sick friends to be healed. There's no mention here of the Savior having a nap after lunch. It was still the Sabbath so they could not carry those who were ill until the sun set. That would be considered work and they weren't supposed to work on the Sabbath.

Whenever Jesus would cast out demons they would say, "You are the Son of God!" But again, He did not want evil spirits to be His announcers, so He would silence them.

What a kind, but powerful Savior we have!

[See also: Matthew 8:14-17; Mark 1:29-34]

## WHAT DO YOU THINK?

1. What is another title for Satan that we discussed?

2. Why didn't Jesus allow the evil spirits to announce who He was, since they were telling the truth?

3. When Jesus was performing many miracles—something no one else could do—why do you think that the Jews did not immediately recognize that He was the promised Messiah and immediately crown Him King of the Jews.

## ANSWERS TO YOUR QUESTIONS

1. *Satan (or the devil) is also called "the father of lies."*

2. *Jesus did not want these evil spirits, who constantly deceived and lied to the people in trying to destroy them, to announce Jesus as the Son of God.*

3. *Personal opinion. You may want to ask each child. Below are several reasons:*
   - *They had known Him since He was a child.*
   - *They were probably expecting the Messiah to be a powerful conqueror who would free them from the Romans.*
   - *Their sin had clouded their minds and hearts.*
   - *They didn't know their own Old Testament Scriptures.*

*Learning to trust Jesus*

## 17. A GOOD DAY'S FISHING

*And when He had finished speaking, He said to Simon, "Put out into the deep water and let down your nets for a catch."...And when they had done this, they enclosed a great quantity of fish; and their nets began to break.*
*Luke 5:4, 6*

Have you ever run into a school of decent sized fish where everyone in your group had a fish on their line at the same time? During our time as missionaries in Panama, Central America, I went fishing several times in the Panama Canal (specifically Lake Gatun). There were usually four of us in a boat and when we came across a school of peacock bass, we could all catch one every ten minutes. We would then go in to shore where a young Panamanian boy would fillet the fish for us and we would head for home with a cooler full of bass fillets.

Jesus was constantly teaching His disciples, and most of the lessons dealt with their need to trust Him in every area all the time. It's interesting to notice Peter's reaction when Jesus guided all those fish toward Peter's boat. "But when Simon Peter saw that, he fell down at Jesus' feet, saying, 'Depart from me, for I am a sinful man, O Lord!' For amazement had seized him and all his companions because of the catch of fish which they had taken..." (Luke 5:8, 9).

Do you think the big fisherman really wanted Jesus to leave him? I think he was aware of his inability to provide his own needs, and how powerfully able Jesus was, and so he was deeply humbled. He didn't feel worthy to even be in the presence of the Son of God.

Notice that Peter still had to obey Jesus and take his boat out into the deeper water. But Peter had to stop relying on his own years of experience as a fisherman and obey his master. Can you imagine if Peter had said, "In all due respect, Lord, you are a carpenter. I grew up fishing this lake and if there is one thing I know, it's how to catch fish"?

Jesus was about to teach Peter and His other disciples how to "catch men, women, and children" and lead them to the Savior.

[See also: Matthew 4:18-22; Mark 1:16-20]

## WHAT DO YOU THINK?

1. Have you ever run into a school of fish and been able to catch one after another? What was your greatest fishing experience ever?

2. What do you call it when you feel you have so much experience in an area that you no longer need anyone's help—including God's?

3. You would think Peter would have been jumping up and down when he caught all those fish. How did he react and why?

∞

## ANSWERS TO YOUR QUESTIONS

1. *Personal opinion. You may want to ask each child.*

2. *Pride—and foolishness.*

3. *Peter fell down at Jesus' feet and according to Luke 5:8 said, "Depart from me, for I am a sinful man, O Lord!" Apparently he saw his own pride and also how powerful the Lord was—further proof that He was the Messiah they had been waiting for.*

*Healed by faith*

## 18. THE LEPER WHO TRUSTED JESUS

*And it came about that while He was in one of the cities, behold, there was a man full of leprosy; and when he saw Jesus, he fell on his face and implored [begged] Him, saying, "Lord, if You are willing, You can make me clean."*
                    Luke 5:12

I would like to introduce you to a wonderful Christian doctor. His name was Dr. Paul Brand, and he was a world expert on leprosy before he passed away.

Dr. Brand grew up as a missionary's child in India where his parents lived with and cared for the very poor Kollie Malai people. Even as a child, Paul Brand saw many tribal people with stubs of fingers and toes, which they had lost to leprosy. Years later—during the Second World War—Paul went to medical school in England where he became a specialist in hand surgery and leprosy. Soon after the war ended, he returned to India and the people he loved so much.

Prior to Dr. Brand's time, the thinking among scientists was that leprosy itself destroyed the fingers and toes. Through Paul's study of pain, he was able to prove that those with the disease lost all feeling in these areas, and when they got cut or infected, they didn't take proper care of them—they had no feeling there at all. Some would even pick hot coals out of their cooking fire.[2]

Jesus healed many lepers when He was on earth. We read about one of them in today's verse. This man "full of leprosy" who Jesus met along the way, demonstrates the true meaning of faith. First of all, he was *humble*. By falling at Jesus' feet, he was admitting that he was unable to help himself, and he had found the only One who could cure him.

Second, when he called Jesus "Lord," he was also saying, "You are the Messiah—the beloved Son of God."

And finally, he stated his confidence in Jesus' power to heal him—"if You are willing, You can make me clean."

Jesus so appreciated this diseased man's faith that He said, "I am willing; be cleansed."

[See also: Matthew 8:2-4; Mark 1:40-45]

## WHAT DO YOU THINK?

1. What did Dr. Paul Brand discover about the effect of leprosy on people's fingers and toes?

2. What kind of attitude did the man with leprosy have?

3. How did the leper show his faith in Jesus' ability to heal him?

## ANSWERS TO YOUR QUESTIONS

*1. He discovered that leprosy didn't cause the diseased people's fingers and toes to fall off. Rather, they lost all feeling there, and when their fingers and toes were cut or burned and became infected, they would eventually lose them.*

*2. When the leprous man fell down at Jesus' feet, he showed humility before the Son of God.*

*3. He showed faith in Jesus by what he said: "Lord, if You are willing, You can make me clean."*

## 19. JESUS' INVITATION—"FOLLOW ME!"

*And after that He went out, and noticed a tax-gatherer named Levi, sitting in the tax office, and He said to him, "Follow Me." And he left everything behind, and rose and began to follow Him.*
Luke 5:27, 28

What would cause a person to close the door to a very lucrative [wealth producing] business and never go back to it? To get the full impact of the story, let's examine what this business was.

Levi, later called Matthew (the gift of God) by Jesus, was a tax-gatherer. During the time that Jesus walked this earth, the Roman government assigned certain Jews to collect taxes from the people of Israel.

These tax-gatherers were hated by their own people for several reasons:
- They were Jews collecting money from their fellow-Jews, to give to the hated Romans.
- The Romans were the conquerors over Israel, so it was like supporting the enemy.
- Undoubtedly they gathered more than they were required to, and kept the extra for themselves. They were getting wealthy by stealing from their own countrymen.

Jesus apparently saw the radical change in Matthew's heart as he trusted in the Savior, and so he invited this hated man to be His disciple. The Lord simply said, "Follow Me!" That's all Matthew needed. He closed his office door, and Luke reports, he "left everything behind." That must have included the Roman tax money and his own profits.

One of the first things Matthew did to show his new heart change, was to throw a huge banquet for his tax-gathering coworkers, for Jesus, His disciples, and apparently some Pharisees and scribes. I'm sure he wanted to introduce Jesus to his old friends.

Isn't it interesting the changes that take place in a person's heart, when he trusts Jesus to be his Savior? In Matthew's case, he no longer thought only about how much money he could collect—

he just wanted to follow the Son of God and live to please Him. Matthew immediately left the "tax business" and became a "fisher of men."

[See also: Matthew 9:9-17; Mark 2:13-22]

## WHAT DO YOU THINK?

1. What did Levi, later called Matthew, do for a living?

2. Why was Matthew hated so much by his fellow Jews?

3. What was there in Matthew's response that indicated he not only believed in Christ, but he also experienced a life change?

## ANSWERS TO YOUR QUESTIONS

1. *Matthew was a Jew who collected taxes for the Roman government from his fellow countrymen.*

2. *First of all, the people of Israel were forced to pay him their taxes and no one usually likes to do that. Next, the money was going to the Roman government—the conqueror and enemy of Israel. Finally, most tax-gatherers at that time charged the people extra and kept that for themselves.*

3. *Matthew left everything behind in his tax office and immediately followed Jesus. He then put on a banquet where his fellow tax-gatherers and friends could meet Jesus the Messiah.*

## 20. OUCH! I THINK I NEED A DOCTOR

*And Jesus answered and said to them, "It is not those who are well who need a physician, but those who are sick. I have not come to call the righteous but sinners to repentance."*
Luke 5:31, 32

Some people are deathly afraid of doctors and hospitals. I don't remember ever feeling that way. When I am seriously hurting or ill, I can't wait to have an experienced doctor relieve my pain.

A few days before this past Christmas—actually the same day as our wedding anniversary—I began to develop severe pain below my ribs on the right side. When I couldn't stand the pain anymore, I told my wife, "We've got to go to the hospital!"

The ER staff did a lot of tests, and by the next morning, they were sure my gall bladder had to come out. A pre-operation nurse prepared me for surgery which included signing a lot of papers. The last step was to talk to the surgeon who would be operating on me.

So, there we were! I was lying on a metal table on wheels with my wife standing at my side. Suddenly around the corner came a young man who appeared to be about eighteen. He didn't look like he even shaved yet. I felt like asking him, "Does your mother know you're here?" My wife's eyes were so wide she barely blinked. He announced, "I'm Dr. Smith and I'm going to be doing your surgery—do you have any questions?"

Del barely missed a beat. She blurted out, 'How old are you?" Well, it turned out he was thirty-three years old and well qualified, but we all had a good laugh—even the doctor.

Yes, people who are very sick or in pain go to a doctor. Jesus talked about that to make a very important point in today's story. The Pharisees and scribes who were eating at Matthew's house along with Jesus and His disciples, could not understand why this so-called Messiah would eat at the same table with "sinners"—those who collected taxes and stole some for themselves. Jesus' response hit the bull's-eye! He explained that He came into the world to save those who realized they were sinful and without hope. Self-righteous people like the Pharisees believed they were almost perfect—so why would they need a savior?

The Son of God can't help those people who insist they have done enough good deeds to deserve heaven. But He will save for all eternity those men, women, and young people who believe that Christ died and rose again to pay their sin-debt.

When do we need a doctor? When we are seriously ill. When do we need a savior? If we've never put our trust in Jesus Christ, the answer is *right now!*

[See also: Matthew 9:12, 13; Mark 2:17]

## WHAT DO YOU THINK?

1. How did the Pharisees feel about those who collected taxes for the Romans?

2. Why do you think the scribes (the experts on the Law of Moses) and the Pharisees didn't feel they had a personal need for a savior like Jesus?

3. Why would Jesus choose to associate with those who were poor, sickly, and despised by others as sinners?

## ANSWERS TO YOUR QUESTIONS

1. *The Pharisees considered the tax-gatherers to be "sinners." Because they collected taxes from their own people, the Jews, and stole some on the side, they obviously needed saving.*

2. *The scribes and Pharisees were proud and felt they were better than most people. After all, they studied the Law of Moses and deceived themselves into thinking that they obeyed it all and therefore were not sinners like others.*

3. *Just like a physician prefers to help people who are truly sick, so Jesus sought out those who realized they were sinners in need of a savior. Although He came to save the whole world, He could only help those willing to admit they had a real need.*

*Dependence on God*

## 21. IS "MORE" PRAYER ALWAYS BETTER? .

*And it was at this time that He went off to the mountain to pray, and He spent the whole night in prayer to God. And when day came, He called His disciples to Him; and chose twelve of them, whom He also named as apostles.*
*Luke 6:12, 13*

Can you imagine praying all night? How would you ever stay awake? What would you say to God all that time?

We don't have a lot of details in Luke and Mark where we find this story. What we do know is that Jesus was about to choose twelve men out of the crowds of people who followed Him, and He wanted to spend plenty of time with His Father talking about it.

Prayer is not a marathon or an endurance race. I don't believe God's attitude toward prayer is that if one hour of prayer is good, then six hours is fantastic. In other words, He doesn't measure the value of our times of talking with Him with a stop watch. Our "attitude" towards prayer is most important.

Prayer is part of our love relationship with our heavenly Father. He wants to develop a deep friendship with those who are His children. He already knows us—He wants us to get to know Him.

One thing that keeps us from praying is the sin of *independence.* Most of us think we can handle important decisions ourselves without anyone else's help. Wouldn't you say that at times we even get upset when someone tries to tell us what to do or how to do it?

It's a great lesson for us when we see Jesus, who is God Himself, still getting alone with His Father, to discuss the important decision ahead of Him—like choosing twelve disciples out of possibly hundreds of followers.

God obviously wants His children to be dependent on Him. Why? Because He knows what the very best choice is; He knows everything. When we are independent of Him we often make the wrong choices.

Aren't we fortunate to have a heavenly Father like that?
[See also: Matthew 10:1-4; Mark 3:13-19]

## WHAT DO YOU THINK?

1. What important decision was Jesus facing at this time?

2. If the *length* of time that we pray isn't the most important factor, what is?

3. Since God the Father already knows everything, why does He encourage us to come to Him to discuss our lives and choices?

## ANSWERS TO YOUR QUESTIONS

1. *Jesus was about to choose twelve disciples from the crowds of followers and He wanted to do His Father's will.*

2. *Our "heart attitude" is more important than the length of time we pray.*

3. *Several reasons why God the Father wants us to pray: He wants to give His children what is the very best for them; God already knows us—He wants us to get to know Him; and He knows that if we are independent of Him it will hurt us.*

*Criticism*

## 22. THERE'S A LOG IN MY EYE

*"And why do you look at the speck that is in your brother's eye, but do not notice the log that is in your own eye?...You hypocrite, first take the log out of your own eye, and then you will see clearly to take out the speck that is in your brother's eye."*
*Luke 6:41, 42*

I have some specks in my eyes! They are called "floaters" and they are like little grains of sand in the fluid inside my eyes. The difference is that they don't stay still, but every time I blink, they move from side to side. It was a little spooky at first, because one day I suddenly became aware of these microscopic "sail boats" floating slowly across my vision.

Floaters aren't usually dangerous and they aren't painful. They are actually common in people over fifty years of age. After you get over the strangeness of these specks, you hardly ever notice them. There really isn't any way of treating them medically.

But this isn't what Jesus was talking about here, is it? And He's also not saying that I shouldn't have opinions about other people's behavior. It's what I do with those opinions that concern our Savior.

When a friend or relative acts in a harmful or sinful way, I have a responsibility before God to mention it to him, as an act of love. The Lord asks me to take one important step before I take the person aside privately and mention what I see—prayerfully examine my own motive or reason for talking to the person about their fault. Could I be jealous or angry at the person for some reason? Do I just want to look better myself? Or maybe I want to put the person down because "I don't like them."

Jesus is obviously exaggerating when He talks about a speck of sawdust in your friend's eye (their fault) and a two-by-four in your eye (your attitude toward them) to teach a lesson.

If when you pray about it, the Lord shows you that your heart is right and you are genuinely concerned about the other person, then talk to them one-on-one in a kind way. You might be amazed at how the Lord will work in their heart—and in your friendship as well.

[See also: Matthew 7:1-5; Romans 14:10]

## WHAT DO YOU THINK?

1. Is Jesus saying in this lesson that we should never have an opinion about other people's attitudes and actions?

2. Why is it important to prayerfully determine first what our own motive is before pointing out another person's sin or harmful behavior?

3. If the Lord Jesus gives us a peace in our hearts to talk to a friend about their need, what would be a good way to go about it?

༺༻

## ANSWERS TO YOUR QUESTIONS

1. *No! However Jesus is concerned with what we do with that opinion.*

2. *It could be that our own reason for thinking the way we do about another person, is just as wrong—or maybe even worse. The Lord, who lives in us, can easily show us.*

3. *We should first prayerfully examine our own motives or reasons for talking to the person about their fault. If our motive is the other person's benefit, then we should go and talk with them one-on-one in a kind way.*

*Bearing spiritual fruit*

## 23. AN APPLE TREE ALWAYS GROWS APPLES

*"For each tree is known by its own fruit."*
Luke 6:44

If you and I were suddenly dropped into Jerusalem during Jesus' days on earth, we probably would not have been best buddies with the Pharisees. You may think that's odd because they were the most "religious" people in their world. They would stand out from the others because they dressed alike, were constantly saying prayers, and reading from the Old Testament.

But wouldn't that be good? Not really, since it's not what we *say* we are, or how we *dress* that's important. It's what comes out of our lives! For example, let's look at an average Pharisee in the crowd that followed Jesus. Luke describes him like this:

PROUD – They constantly challenged what Jesus said and did, as He preached to the multitudes. Why? Because the Lord did not follow their version of the Old Testament law. They didn't understand that the Law was all about Jesus, the Son of God.

CRITICAL – The only reason the Pharisees followed Jesus was because they were critical and wanted to find some fault in Him, so they could eliminate Him. The Pharisees said to Jesus, "Why do you do what is not lawful on the Sabbath" (Luke 6:2)? Jesus called them hypocrites [a hypocrite is someone who claims to believe something, and then acts the opposite way].

HATEFUL – Jesus was loving, and He constantly healed the sick and helped people. The Pharisees were unwilling to admit that Jesus was the long-awaited Messiah. Luke writes, "But they themselves were filled with rage, and discussed together what they might do to Jesus" (Luke 6:11).

What did Jesus mean when He said that each tree is "known by its own fruit"? An apple tree will always produce apples—never bananas. Similarly, a grape vine will never grow poison ivy. The fruit that grows comes from the "heart" of the tree.

So it is that the loving and kind qualities of Jesus' character can only be seen in a person, if He is living in that person's heart. If a person has never trusted in the Son of God, the only "fruit" produced will come from their old nature, like anger, pride, and jealousy.

What kind of "tree" are you, and what kind of "fruit" do you produce?

[See also: Matthew 7:16-20; James 3:12]

## WHAT DO YOU THINK?

1. What is a Pharisee?

2. What kind of "fruit" was produced in the life of a typical Pharisee? Why?

3. How is "good fruit" produced in a person's life?

## ANSWERS TO YOUR QUESTIONS

*1. A Pharisee was a man who, during Jesus' time on earth, belonged to a religious order or group. They claimed that they constantly studied the Old Testament Law, and because of their "religious behavior," were better or more righteous than the average Jew. They also added their own rules to God's Law and were critical of those who didn't follow them.*

*2. The fruit or behavior that came from a typical Pharisee was what comes from our fleshly old nature: jealousy, hatred, envy, pride, criticism, and greed. Because they did not trust in Jesus, the Messiah, that's the only fruit they could produce.*

*3. First, a person needs to realize she is a sinner and then believe that Jesus took her place on the cross to pay her "sin debt." She also needs to believe that Jesus was buried and rose again "alive," to return to God the Father in heaven (See 1 Corinthians 15:1-4). Then the fruit produced in her life comes from Jesus' life within her.*

## 24. THE BEST FOUNDATION

*"And why do you call Me, 'Lord, Lord,' and do not do what I say?"*
*Luke 6:46*

How would you feel if your closest friend, who was always friendly and kind to you when you were together, talked about you in negative and hurtful ways when you weren't around? Wouldn't you feel betrayed—even lied to?

Now let's consider ourselves. Do we talk and act like obedient Christians when certain people are around, but then act just like an unbeliever when we are with unsaved friends? The Lord certainly does not approve of that kind of lifestyle for His children. He knows how destructive it is for believers to behave like unbelievers, and He would never say, "I'm fine with My children living two different lives—one way with Christians and another way with unbelievers. I know how hard it is being a Christian and living in our complicated world."

I can't imagine the Lord feeling that way at all. He knows how destructive it can be for His children to live like unbelievers. Why then would He approve of us living like that?

In today's verses in Luke, we look in on Jesus' teaching this very principle, where He compares it to building a house on sand and building on solid rock.

A few years ago, there were horrible floods in Central Wisconsin. As the rivers filled with rushing torrents, the riverbanks began falling into the swirling waters. Beautiful homes stood along the banks of a particular river, but they were built too close to the edge. The banks disappeared into the rising waters, and gaping holes appeared under the foundations of the homes. Finally, the bank eroded so much that half of the house hung out over the river. Within hours, these beautiful waterfront homes tipped over and fell into the raging waters, bobbing downstream like houseboats. The owners had built their homes on the sand.

Jesus said, "But the one who has heard, and has not acted accordingly, is like a man who built a house upon the ground without any foundation; and the torrent [flood] burst against it and immediately it collapsed, and the ruin of that house was great" (Luke 6:49).

The Lord Jesus compares a person who talks like a Christian, but doesn't obey the Lord to just such a house. Eventually their phony words will prove that they are all *talk* and no *walk*. On the other hand, a Christian who chooses to obey God and His Word, will stand strong like a house built on rock—even when a hurricane comes.

[See also: Matthew 7:21-23]

## WHAT DO YOU THINK?

1. Read today's verse again and explain it in your own words.

2. To what does Jesus compare a person who obeys God and His Word?

3. Jesus compares a Christian who does not obey Him to a house built on sand that collapses when a storm comes along. What could such a Christian's life look like?

## ANSWERS TO YOUR QUESTIONS

*1. Personal opinion. You may want to ask each child.*

*2. Jesus compares such a person to a house that is built on a firm foundation of rock.*

*3. Personal opinion. You could build a composite picture with the comments of each of your children.*

*Worthy of Christ's love?*

## 25. THE SOLDIER WHO LOVED HIS SERVANT

*And when they had come to Jesus, they earnestly entreated Him, saying, "He [the centurion] is worthy for You to grant this to him"...the centurion sent friends, saying to Him [Jesus], "Lord, do not trouble Yourself further, for I am not worthy for You to come under my roof."*

*Luke 7:4, 6*

These verses tell the story of a great friendship between a centurion (a Roman army officer over 100 soldiers), and his faithful servant. Even more than that, we read of this centurion's humility and his trust in Jesus.

Here was a man of wealth and authority who helped the Roman army overpower the land of Israel and its Jewish citizens. Yet somehow he had heard of this worker of miracles, Jesus, and he put his trust in Him to not only heal his servant, but also meet his own heart need.

The centurion sent some Jewish elders (religious leaders) to Jesus, asking Him to come and "save the life of his slave." Notice their words to Jesus: "For he [the centurion] is *worthy* for you to grant this to him." These elders were looking at the situation just like an unbeliever would. They were thinking, "The centurion is a man of power and reputation—surely this carpenter from Nazareth who hangs out with fishermen, ought to beat a path to his door to help him."

But that wasn't the attitude of the Roman officer. When Jesus was close to the soldier's house, the centurion sent friends out to meet Jesus, and his words were very different. He remarked that someone as great as Jesus, should not trouble Himself—He should not stoop so low—as to come to his house. Why not, since his slave was deathly ill? Because he, even though an officer over one hundred men, was still not *worthy* to have the Son of God visit him.

Why was Jesus willing to travel to this soldier's house? Because the man humbled himself and realized that he was not worthy to host the Jewish Messiah. And that's what grace is all about. No man, woman, or child is worthy to receive God's gift of salvation. To be worthy of something means that you have rightfully earned it—like a week's salary. No one deserves to go to heaven, since we are all sinners. That's why God the Father sent His Son, Jesus, to earth, to die on the cross—because as Romans 3:23 says, "...for all have sinned and fall short [are not worthy] of the glory of God..."

Grace means that God had to provide a way to heaven for a world of people who deserved only hell. The Bible states the good news clearly, "For the wages [payment] of sin is death, but the free gift of God [grace] is eternal life in Christ Jesus our Lord" (Romans 6:23).

The centurion in today's story understood grace—that he was not worthy of Jesus—and so the Savior came to him, with the wonderful free gift of eternal life.

[See also: Matthew 8:5-13]

## WHAT DO YOU THINK?

1. Why was it strange that the centurion would pay any attention to Jesus?

2. Why do you think Jesus healed the centurion's slave?

3. What does "grace" mean, and how does it apply in today's story?

---

## ANSWERS TO YOUR QUESTIONS

1. *The centurion was a Roman army officer, wealthy and powerful, and part of the conquering Roman army that dominated Israel and its Jewish population. Jesus would be considered a common laborer—a carpenter from the backwoods town of Nazareth.*

2. *Jesus knew the motive of the centurion's heart. Although the Lord appeared like a common carpenter, this army officer somehow realized He was the Messiah of Israel with authority over diseases, and he trusted Him.*

3. *Grace means that God provided a way to be saved and to go to heaven for men, women, and children who deserved only hell because of their sin. Salvation is a free gift from God to those who believe in Jesus. It appears that the centurion realized that Jesus was the Messiah sent from God—probably because of His miracles. He knew he didn't deserve the Lord's help, but he asked in faith.*

## 26. WHAT AMAZES YOU?

*Now when Jesus heard this, He marveled [was amazed] at him, and turned and said to the multitude that was following Him, "I say to you, not even in Israel have I found such great faith."*
*Luke 7:9*

As long as I can remember, I have been totally amazed by illusionists or as some people call them, "magicians." One of the most famous in my lifetime is David Copperfield, who didn't just settle for card tricks, but preferred illusions on a grand scale. Television helped to give him an audience of millions.

One particular "trick" that no one else has attempted, was to appear to walk through the Great Wall of China in 1986. I remember watching it on TV, and I was totally amazed. As best as I could see, he walked into the side of the wall and came out the other side. In my mind I knew it was impossible, but still it seems like I saw him do it. Three years earlier, David Copperfield appeared to make the Statue of Liberty disappear. Utterly amazing!

Did you know that the Bible records two occasions when Jesus was amazed? One of them occurs in today's verses (and in Matthew 8:10), where Jesus is deeply moved that a Gentile army officer would humble himself before Him. The soldier trusted that the Lord could miraculously heal his slave.

The other time when Jesus was amazed was when He preached in His hometown of Nazareth. Mark writes, "And He [Jesus] was amazed at their lack of faith (NIV)" (Mark 6:6).

This Roman soldier in today's verse recognized that he was not worthy to ask any favors of Jesus, and yet, because of his love and respect for his slave, he urged the Lord to come and heal him.

It helps to remember that since Jesus was God as well as man, He knew the centurion's thoughts long in advance. However, it was such a rare event to find a Gentile with that kind of trust, that Jesus really was God's Messiah, that He makes sure it is recorded in Scripture.

It still delights and maybe even amazes the Lord, when people like you and I trust Him fully in difficult situations.

## WHAT DO YOU THINK?

1. What kind of attitude did the Roman centurion have toward his slave? What does this tell us about his character?

2. At what two situations that were opposite of each other, was Jesus amazed?

3. Can you think of one aspect of Jesus' personality that amazes you?

## ANSWERS TO YOUR QUESTIONS

1. *The centurion appeared to care deeply for his slave and was concerned enough when his slave got deathly ill, to get help for him. This army officer must have been a very kind man who wanted to help others and not just himself.*

2. *The Bible describes two situations where we're told that Jesus marveled or was amazed. In the case of the people of Nazareth, it was their "unbelief," while with the centurion, Jesus was amazed at his faith or trust.*

3. *Personal opinion. You may want to ask each child.*

*Jesus is the "Expected One"*

## 27. DO WE LOOK FOR SOMEONE ELSE?

*And when the men had come to Him, they said, "John the Baptist has sent us to You, saying, 'Are You the Expected One, or do we look for someone else?'"*
*Luke 7:20*

In the C. S. Lewis book, *The Silver Chair,* of the Narnia series, there is an awesome scene between a young girl named Jill, and the lion, Aslan. As Jill is walking in the woods, she becomes very thirsty and happens upon a stream. Unfortunately there is a lion between her and the refreshing water. She is afraid to run for fear that the lion will chase her, and yet in order to get a drink of water, she has to pass this fierce looking beast. As we used to say when we were younger, "She's in a real pickle!"

The lion asks Jill if she's thirsty, and of course she answers that she is. He invites her to drink. The young girl is frightened to approach any closer, and the lion rightly concludes that she will die of thirst if she doesn't.

"Oh, dear!" said Jill, coming another step nearer. "I suppose I must go and look for another stream then."

*"There is no other stream!"* said the lion.[3]

In today's verses, John the Baptist sent his disciples to Jesus to ask if He was the long-awaited Messiah of Israel. Since God first made His promise to Abraham in Genesis 12:3 that a descendant of his would be a blessing to "all the families of the earth," the Jewish nation had waited for their deliverer. Now it appeared that He had finally come in the person of Jesus of Nazareth.

Can you imagine John's excitement as he urged his followers to go and ask this miracle-worker if He was the One who all Israel looked for? When these eager young men said to the Lord, "...do we look for someone else?" Jesus could have rightly said, "There is no one else!" Jesus said, "I am the way, and the truth, and the life; no one comes to the Father, but through Me" (John 14:6).

[See also: Matthew 11:1-19]

## WHAT DO YOU THINK?

1. Who does the lion most likely represent in this story from *"The Silver Chair"*? How about Jill?

2. What was the significance of the lion's statement, "There is no other stream"?

3. Explain in your own words the question that John's disciples brought to Jesus.

## ANSWERS TO YOUR QUESTIONS

1. *The lion in the story most likely represents Jesus Christ, who is called in Revelation 5:5, "...the Lion that is from the tribe of Judah..." Jill represents all of mankind—lost and in need of the Living Water.*

2. *Jesus Christ is the one and only way to be saved and to go to heaven. There are many religions and cults in the world that promise eternal life through other gods. However, as God's Word states clearly in John 14:6, there is no other "stream" or way of salvation except through Jesus Christ.*

3. *Personal opinion.*

*Repentance involves worshiping Jesus*

## 28. THE SWEET AROMA OF REPENTANCE

*And behold, there was a woman in the city who was a sinner; and when she learned that He was reclining at the table in the Pharisee's house, she brought an alabaster vial of perfume, and standing behind Him at His feet, weeping, she began to wet His feet with her tears, and kept wiping them with the hair of her head, and kissing His feet, and anointing them with the perfume.*
*Luke 7:37, 38*

One day Jesus was invited for a meal to the house of a Pharisee named Simon. Thanks to Dr. Luke, we have a wonderful picture of repentance, humility, and forgiveness—we also get a pretty good illustration of pride.

What a shock it must have been to Simon when a woman with an immoral (sinful) reputation, suddenly walked into his house and stood at Jesus' feet. She was obviously not invited and, after all, who would invite a person with such a terrible background anyway? Simon had a reputation of religiously keeping the Law, and no religious person would invite such a creature. What must Simon's guests think?

But the host did not know Jesus very well—in fact, it's pretty clear he didn't know the Lord at all. Jesus, being God the Son, knew the thoughts of both Simon and the woman.

Picture all the guests and Simon reclining at the dinner table on couches—their feet away from the food while they lean a forearm on the table and eat. All the guests are in a state of shock, looking to see what Simon will do—all except Jesus.

The woman stops at Jesus, weeping over His feet, wiping them with her hair, kissing them, and anointing His feet with an expensive perfume. Was Jesus offended? Not at all, because He knew that she had trusted in Him as her Savior. She was overwhelmed that all her sin had been forgiven, and worshiped the Son of God the only way she knew—with tears of repentance and thankfulness.

And how about Simon? All he could do was find fault with Jesus for His association with a "sinful" person.

Don't you just love the way the Lord Jesus is so forgiving to those who genuinely recognize their sin?

## WHAT DO YOU THINK?

1. Simon the Pharisee was correct that the woman was a sinner. What did he fail to see in her that Jesus saw?

2. Wouldn't you think Jesus would be embarrassed to have a stranger act the way the woman did, in front of all of Simon's guests? Why wouldn't He tell her to stop?

3. What was missing in Simon's life that obviously existed in the life of the woman?

## ANSWERS TO YOUR QUESTIONS

1. *Simon was taken up with his own religious reputation of being a "good person." He looked at the woman as a "bad person" because of her past history. Jesus recognized that she had trusted in Him for salvation and she was overwhelmed that all her sins had been forgiven. She only wanted to worship her Savior.*

2. *Jesus was far more interested in the woman's faith, in His forgiveness of her sins, and her worshipful, thankful attitude toward Him, than how He would look to others.*

3. *Because Simon was convinced of his own goodness, he saw no need of a savior. The woman, on the other hand, had come to realize she was a lost sinner, humbled herself by trusting in Christ, and was moved to tears by the Lord's forgiveness.*

*Christ loves to forgive sins*

## 29. FORGIVEN MUCH AND LITTLE

*"For this reason I say to you, her sins, which are many, have been forgiven, for she loved much; but he who is forgiven little, loves little." And He said to her, "Your sins have been forgiven."*
*Luke 7:47, 48*

The largest church in the world is in South Korea—we'll call the pastor, Pastor Kim. During the Second World War, the Japanese had treated the Koreans cruelly, and it left a hatred for the people of Japan in the hearts of many Koreans—including Pastor Kim.

Along the way, he was invited to speak to a group of one thousand pastors in Japan, and he accepted. When Pastor Kim first opened his mouth, the words that came tumbling out were, "I hate you! I hate you! I hate you!" And then he broke down sobbing in humility before his audience.

One after another of the Japanese pastors came forward and at Pastor Kim's feet confessed their guilt as a nation for having treated the Korean people so badly. The Lord changed the heart of Pastor Kim also as he confessed the hatred and bitterness in his own heart. His message then to the Japanese people became, "I love you! I love you! I love you!"[4]

On this occasion of the dinner at Simon the Pharisee's house, Jesus was using this opportunity to teach about *forgiveness*. Simon felt he was an extremely righteous "man of the cloth," so he didn't really need much forgiveness—well maybe just a speck. After all, nobody's perfect. In reality he was proud and self-righteous—and lost!

The immoral woman, on the other hand, knew clearly she was a sinner. Surely she was reminded of it every night that she walked the streets. But there was something very different about her. She was broken, humbled, and probably hating her sin. In reality, both Simon and the woman were equally sinners before God. The difference was that the woman saw she couldn't forgive her own sin, and so she ran to the mercy and forgiveness of the Savior. Luke doesn't record her saying a single word.

How did Jesus set her heart free? With these simple words: "Your sins have been forgiven…your faith has saved you; go in peace" (Luke 7:48, 50).

## WHAT DO YOU THINK?

1. What were Pastor Kim's first words to the Japanese pastors? Why did he feel that way? What happened then?

2. What was Simon the Pharisee's attitude toward Jesus? How did he compare himself to the uninvited guest?

3. Although there is no record of the woman saying a single word, why did Jesus say to her, "Your sins have been forgiven"?

## ANSWERS TO YOUR QUESTIONS

*1. Pastor Kim told the pastors he hated them, because of the cruel treatment of the Korean people at the hands of the Japanese army during World War 2. He then broke down in tears of repentance, realizing that his heart was full of bitterness.*

*2. Simon proudly felt that he was a very religious person—after all he was a Pharisee. So, he thought that he did not need Jesus' forgiveness. Also, he looked down on God's Son for having anything to do with this "sinner."*

*3. Jesus could not only see into her mind that she was broken up about her sin, but her actions of kindness and thankfulness to Him, demonstrated what had taken place in her heart.*

*Faith in God's Word pleases Him*

## 30. THE POWER OF TRUST

*"And the seed in the good soil, these are the ones who have heard the word in an honest and good heart, and hold it fast, and bear fruit with perseverance."*
*Luke 8:15*

When our children were young, we decided to plant the seeds of a particularly tasty watermelon in our backyard. Some never came out of the ground at all, and we suspect some squirrels got them. Others began to grow, but shriveled up in time and never came close to producing any melons. We put them out of their misery. A few, however, responded to the rain and the sun, and began to shoot runners along the ground. Soon there were little green marbles that became baseball-size fruit, and one day—toward the end of summer—there were actual mature watermelons. They were nothing like the ones you see in the stores, but they were *ours* and we enjoyed the fruit of our labors.

As Jesus looked at the crowds who followed Him, He realized that not all of the people received what He said, trusted Him as their Savior, and became changed in their hearts. In this parable (a story with a lesson), the four kinds of soil represent people's hearts and their responses to His teaching. The seed is God's Word, and the sower (planter) is God's servant.

The disciples had trouble getting the point of the four soils, so the Lord explained that they represented the *hard* heart, the *shallow* heart, the *crowded* heart, and the *fruitful* heart.[5]

Today's verse describes the fourth type of soil—or the heart that receives God's Word by faith and is born again. As this true believer in Christ begins to grow, she shows evidence of the new spiritual life within her heart.

When our family grew the watermelons, we planted all the seeds in identical ways. There was no problem with the seeds and they all received the same amount of rain and sun. The amount of growth was dependent on the soil because even in that one garden there was hard clay, sand, and rich top soil.

In the same manner, our hearts respond to God's Word in different ways. The Lord Jesus wants us to simply believe His

Word, because we trust Him—and then He will take care of the fruit growing.

[See also: Matthew 13:1-23; Mark 4:1-20]

## WHAT DO YOU THINK?

1. Have you ever grown a garden? What did you learn personally about watching a seed grow into a plant?

2. When identical seeds are planted that receive the same amount of sun and rain, what primarily determines whether they will grow into healthy, fruit-bearing plants?

3. Describe the last type of soil and what happened to the seed? What point was Jesus making with this example of the fourth soil?

## ANSWERS TO YOUR QUESTIONS

1. *Personal opinion. You may want to ask each child.*

2. *The type of soil is important for the seed to grow. Each seed needs nutrients (basic foods) for its cells to grow and multiply. Without them, the seed stops growing and eventually dries up and dies.*

3. *Jesus called the last type of soil the "good soil," meaning it had the right balance of nutrients and moisture for the seed to grow into a plant and bear fruit. The various types of soil are illustrations of different human responses to hearing the Gospel from God's Word—the condition of their heart and mind.*

*Trust Jesus even in danger!*

## 31. SLEEPING THROUGH THE STORM

*But as they were sailing along He [Jesus] fell asleep; and a fierce gale of wind descended upon the lake, and they began to be swamped and to be in danger...And He said to them, "Where is your faith?"*

*Luke 8:23, 25*

When I was in college, I volunteered with two other men to make up a sailing team, even though I had no previous experience in sailing. The regatta, as these events are called, was held on Lake Ontario in the fall, and the water was frigid. There were at least six other colleges competing and we were definitely the underdog.

Lake Ontario, one of the Great Lakes, is rarely calm, and that particular day the waves were huge. When we started, we didn't know enough about sailing to be afraid. That soon changed as the white caps poured over the sides of the boat, and we found we couldn't bail as fast as the water poured in. Now we were scared!

Fortunately the boat was unsinkable and by the time our vessel had filled with water up to our chests, a launch came along and towed our boat to shore. Some sailors!

I'm sure that Jesus' disciples had similar "sinking feelings." A storm came up quickly on the Sea of Galilee, and they suddenly found themselves bailing out their boat in a state of panic. How could the Lord sleep at a time like this? Apparently Jesus wanted His disciples to learn to trust Him in every situation, especially when He was with them in person. Jesus was at rest because He was in the Father's will—He wanted His followers to have that same confidence that God is bigger and more powerful than any danger.

According to Mark's gospel, the disciples woke up Jesus, the creator of the universe, with the angry question, "...teacher, do You not care that we are perishing" (Mark 4:38)? No one in all of history has cared more for people than the Son of God. After all, He died on Calvary's cross to save mankind because of His loving care.

I can understand the fear that grips your heart when you know your boat is filling with water. But God says, "I will never desert you, nor will I ever forsake you" (Hebrews 13:5).

[See also: Matthew 8:18, 23-27; Mark 4:35-41]

## WHAT DO YOU THINK?

1. Why do you think Jesus took His disciples out on the Sea of Galilee in a sailboat when He knew in advance that there would be a fierce storm?

2. What was the disciples' accusation when they woke Jesus up during the storm?

3. Look up Isaiah 41:10 and explain it in your own words.

## ANSWERS TO YOUR QUESTIONS

1. *Jesus had just healed the centurion's servant to demonstrate to His disciples that as God's Son, He had power over the entire universe—including sickness. Now it was time to test the disciples' faith, to make sure that they would feel secure in every situation of life, including a sinking boat.*

2. *They demanded to know whether Jesus cared for them. Isn't it interesting that in the middle of a dangerous situation, we can forget everything we've learned—we only think of our own safety?*

3. *Personal opinion.*

## 32. FAITH IN GOD IS ALWAYS RIGHT

*And He said to her, "Daughter, your faith has made you well; go in peace..." But when Jesus heard this, He [Jesus] answered him, "Do not be afraid any longer; only believe, and she shall be made well."*

Luke 8:48, 50

At first it seems like these verses in Luke chapter 8 are only about Jesus, two seriously ill people, and their diseases. The sick ones are the twelve-year old daughter of a Jewish official and an unnamed woman. These two stories, though completely separate, seem to be intertwined (braided).

When we look at the stories carefully, we see one common factor that is easily missed. What seems to have urged the Savior to heal this dying girl and the chronically ill woman, was the *faith* involved. Jairus, the girl's father, sought out Jesus, fell at His feet, and pleaded with Him to come to his house. He obviously had seen Jesus perform other miracles of healing. The Bible doesn't say if Jairus actually believed that Christ was the Messiah of Israel and trusted in Him for salvation, but he obviously believed that Jesus was able to heal. That was enough for the Lord to agree to go to the official's home.

Before they could get there, however, a woman who had suffered with a bleeding problem for twelve years and spent all her money, worked her way through the crowd until she could at least grasp Jesus' cloak. When she was finally able to reach out and touch Him, she was healed. Jesus knew it right away and stopped to emphasize to His followers that it was the woman's faith in His power to heal that cured her.

Shortly after this miracle, the Lord accompanied Jairus to his home. As the group headed down the dusty street, friends announced that the young girl had died—there was no longer any need for the "miracle worker." But Jesus is the giver of life as well as the healer of diseases, and He continued on to Jairus' house with words of encouragement for the family: "Do not be afraid any longer; only believe, and she shall be made well."

When Jesus announced to the crowd that had gathered at the house, that Jairus' daughter was only sleeping, His words were met with mocking laughter. Couldn't this teacher from Nazareth see that she was dead? Why give the parents a false hope?

And then with all the power of heaven, Jesus announced, "Child, arise!" Can you imagine how thrilled Jairus and his family were?

Faith in God, as small as it may be, still pleases His great heart!
[See also: Matthew 9:18-26; Mark 5:21-43]

## WHAT DO YOU THINK?

1. What common factor was there in the two healings in today's story?

2. Why do you think Jesus stopped when He sensed that the woman, who had been sick for twelve years, touched His cloak? Surely there were many in the crowd who were touching Him.

3. When the crowd at Jairus' house laughed at the Lord, what did they not understand?

## ANSWERS TO YOUR QUESTIONS

1. *People had faith in Jesus' ability to perform the miracle of healing in both cases.*

2. *Jesus sensed that it was a "teachable moment," and so He used the example of this woman, who only reached out to touch Him, as an example of the faith that pleases Him.*

3. *They did not fully understand that this miracle-worker from Nazareth was the One who created the heavens and earth. He was able to restore life as well as heal diseases.*

## 33. LITTLE IS MUCH, WHEN GOD IS IN IT

*But He said to them, "You give them something to eat!" And they said, "We have no more than five loaves and two fish"...(For there were about five thousand men.)*
Luke 9:13, 14

Have you ever been so busy that you missed a meal? When Jesus' twelve disciples returned from their preaching tour, they were obviously worn out. As the disciples shared their ministry experiences, the Lord sensed that they needed to get alone together to rest. Mark writes, "For there were many people coming and going, and they [disciples] did not even have time to eat." So Jesus urges them to get into a boat to find a lonely place where they could be refreshed.

But the local people wanted to see Jesus perform more miracles—even heal their relatives of serious diseases—so they ran to Bethsaida where the boat was headed. Imagine Jesus and the disciples arriving at their "lonely place," only to find a huge crowd of people waiting for them. Did Jesus say, "Let's go and find some other spot"? Not at all! Jesus felt sorry for the people and saw them like sheep wandering the hills with no shepherd to guide them. Tired as He was, He began to teach them.

When it got to be dinner time, the disciples approached Jesus, encouraging Him to send the people away so they could find food and lodging somewhere. Instead of dismissing the crowd, the Lord said to the Twelve, "You give them something to eat!" The best they could come up with was five barley loaves and two fish belonging to a young lad.

There's a chorus that many children learn in Bible clubs called, *Little Is Much When God Is In It.* That's exactly what took place that day. Jesus gave thanks and then asked the people—probably around 15,000 in total, since there were 5,000 men—to sit on the grass while the disciples passed out the food. Everyone ate until they were satisfied, and there were still twelve baskets of leftovers.

How would the few loaves and fish feed the whole crowd? Because Jesus is God the Son, and by His spoken word, He created the universe. What lesson do you suppose the Lord wanted to teach

His disciples? God wants us to give Him our all—our time, our possessions, our talents—for His use and His glory. We may feel that we don't have much to give Him, but He can take our "five loaves and two fish" and use them as instruments in His powerful hands, to glorify His name. He even rewards us for our faithfulness.

PRAYER: Dear Lord Jesus, You are the all-powerful Son of God as well as being my personal Savior. I give You all that I am and have for Your use and Your glory. Thank You for being my heavenly Father, my Lord, and my King. AMEN.

[See also: Matthew 14:15-21; Mark 6:33-44; John 6:1-14]

## WHAT DO YOU THINK?

1. Even though Jesus was exhausted, how did He see the crowd at Bethsaida when the disciples' boat arrived?

2. What was the disciples' solution to providing food for the crowd of around 15,000 people?

3. Explain in your own words what lesson Jesus was apparently teaching His disciples at this time.

## ANSWERS TO YOUR QUESTIONS

1. *Jesus had compassion (felt sorry for) the crowd gathered at Bethsaida, because they were like sheep wandering on a hillside with no shepherd to care for them and see that they were fed the right things.*

2. *The disciples suggested that Jesus send the crowd away to find a meal and lodging since they didn't see how they could provide enough food.*

3. *Personal opinion. You may want to ask each child. Author's answer: Jesus is able to meet all of our needs. Also, God wants us to give Him our all—our time, our possessions, our talents—for His use and His glory.*

*A disciple takes up his cross*

## 34. WHEN LOSING OUR LIFE MEANS FINDING IT

*And He was saying to them all, "If anyone wishes to come after Me, let him deny himself, and take up his cross daily, and follow Me. For whoever wishes to save his life shall lose it, but whoever loses his life for My sake, he is the one who will save it."*
*Luke 9:23, 24*

When my family lived in the Republic of Panama as missionaries, we saw many cultural differences from the USA. One such difference would occur during the month before Easter. Driving along the Pan American Highway, we would often see young men dressed in bright purple robes, walking alongside the road. Most had a backpack and some used a pole to help them walk.

I never questioned any of these "walkers," but my Panamanian friends explained that these men would often walk 50 or 100 miles in an effort to pay for the sins they had committed. They somehow felt that punishing their bodies like that would convince God to forgive them.

Missionaries in the Philippines have described men who would walk for miles on their knees until they were raw and bloody, for the same reason. Others would beat their bare backs with leather straps until they bled. I heard recently of a man who actually allowed himself to be nailed to a cross, to imitate what Christ did.

Is this what Jesus meant when He said that we should "take up our cross and follow Him"? First of all, Jesus is talking in today's verses about Christians becoming His disciples or obedient followers; He is not referring to them being born again and having their sins forgiven.

To deny ourselves does not mean to just do without certain things that we like. It means to give ourselves as completely as we can to God and His will rather than to choose what will only please us and our own desires. There is often a cost to obeying God's will that includes suffering and even shame—exactly what Jesus experienced on earth. He asks us to be willing to pay that same cost for His glory.

Jesus knew that many people followed Him just to see His miracles. In today's verses He teaches that to be His true followers we need to deny ourselves. That does not mean that we lose our own identity when we become His disciples, but we enter into Christ's life by faith.

The apostle Paul wrote in Romans 12:1, "I urge you therefore, brethren, by the mercies of God, to present your bodies a living and holy sacrifice, acceptable to God, which is your spiritual service of worship." We submit ourselves to God, and He does the "internal work" that's necessary.

You might think, "This is my life and I intend to be the boss of it." I may save my life for myself, but end up being miserable. Taking up our cross may not mean riches in this life, but will definitely mean rewards in heaven.

It sounds like a good deal to me!

[See also: Matthew 16:13-28; Mark 8:27-9:1]

## WHAT DO YOU THINK?

1. Why were the men in Panama wearing purple robes and walking up to 100 miles? Who were they trying to please?

2. When Jesus said that people should take up their cross and follow Him, who was He specifically talking to—believers or unbelievers?

3. What did Jesus mean when He said, "Whosoever loses his life for My sake, he is the one who will save it"?

## ANSWERS TO YOUR QUESTIONS

1. *The men wrongly believe that by punishing their bodies by walking so many miles, that God will forgive the sins they committed during the past year. They were obviously trying to please God.*

2. *Jesus is telling those who believe in Him that if they want to be His true followers or disciples, they should choose to do His will and obey His leading rather than their own.*

3. *If we will do as Romans 12:1, 2 says and present our lives to Jesus for whatever He desires for us, we will experience true joy in this life and rewards when we get to heaven.*

## 35. WHO IS THE GREATEST? WHO'S NUMBER ONE?

*And an argument arose among them as to which of them might be the greatest. But Jesus, knowing what they were thinking in their heart, took a child and stood him by His side, and said to them, "Whoever receives this child in My name receives Me; and whoever receives Me receives Him who sent Me; for he who is least among you, this is the one who is great."*
*Luke 9:46-48*

Our world is obsessed with being number one—the very best in some area in the entire world:
- The boxer Mohammed Ali called himself "the Greatest."
- TV has the "World's Strongest Man" competition.
- The Miss Universe contest supposedly picks the most beautiful and talented woman in the universe—I wonder if they have checked on Mars.
- Albert Einstein is believed to be the smartest human who ever lived—with the exception of Solomon of course.
- Who is the richest man in the world?
- Usain Bolt from Jamaica is currently the fastest man (running) in the world.
- We have all heard sports fans praising their favorite team by saying, "We're number one!"

Do you get the idea? The Guinness Book of World Records is filled with stories of people who risked their lives to be called "number one" in some area. Good-natured competition is helpful for our development—we learn how to win and lose with grace and humility.

Why did Jesus take exception with the disciples who were discussing which of them would be the greatest in the kingdom of heaven? According to verse 46, they were arguing about this matter, which makes you think that they were being proud about it—and pride is sin. The truth is that Jesus is the greatest, but they were too taken up with themselves to think about the Lord. Jesus could see into their hearts, and He could tell that their hearts were not right.

Instead of caring for each other, they were consumed with "being number one."

In order to teach the arguing disciples a lesson in humility, Jesus placed a child next to Him, and said, "Whoever then humbles himself as this child, he is the greatest in the kingdom of heaven" (Matthew 18:4). What did the Lord mean? Children are often trusting, innocent, and willing to simply believe God. If we have the attitude of a servant or of a child, we will put others first before ourselves—we'll be fine with them being number one.

The Lord Jesus was telling the disciples, "Instead of you all arguing over who will be the greatest, adopt the humble attitude of a child—or a servant—and I will raise you to greatness in My kingdom."

I don't think any of us in heaven will be worrying about which of us is the greatest. We'll be too in love with our wonderful Lord Jesus.

[See also: Matthew 18:1-5; Mark 9:33-40]

## WHAT DO YOU THINK?

1. Is it always wrong to want to win in a sports competition? Is it always wrong to want to be the best in the world in some area? What would make it wrong?

2. What were Jesus' disciples discussing? Why did Jesus use it as a "teachable moment"?

3. Besides being argumentative and proud, what was wrong with the disciples discussing who would be the greatest in God's kingdom?

## ANSWERS TO YOUR QUESTIONS

*1. It's not necessarily wrong to be competitive and want to win at something. What makes it wrong is if we are proud and our motive is so that people will give us glory and we can boast about how great we are.*

*2. Jesus' disciples were arguing over who would be the greatest (or number one) in the kingdom of God. Jesus was able to look into their hearts and see the wrong attitudes.*

*3. The disciples were being selfish. Jesus' life and death were all about other people. If they were going to be His followers, they needed to think like their Master.*

## 36. I WANT TO FOLLOW YOU, LORD; BUT FIRST...

*And another also said, "I will follow you, Lord; but first permit me to say good-bye to those at home." But Jesus said to him, "No one, after putting his hand to the plow and looking back, is fit for the kingdom of God."*
Luke 9:61, 62

You can be a Christian without being a disciple of Jesus, but you cannot be His disciple without being a Christian. Does that make sense? Let's think that statement through together.

In verse fifty-one of chapter nine, Luke tells us that Jesus began to focus on traveling to Jerusalem where He knew He would suffer terrible humiliation and eventually be nailed to a cross. I'm sure He wanted to teach His twelve disciples all He could before they would be without Him. And so, the Lord highlights three of His followers who apparently liked being with Him, but weren't prepared to make the things of this world number two, so that Jesus could be number one.

The first was a scribe (a religious Jew who hand-copied the Old Testament Scriptures) according to Matthew 8:19. He announced that he would follow Jesus wherever the Master went. He obviously wasn't aware that Jesus' plan was to go to Calvary. The Lord said that He didn't even own a pillow, let alone His own house. We never hear from the scribe again.

Next, the Lord Jesus Himself approaches a man and invites him to be His follower or disciple (not one of the Twelve). Although the man was most likely part of the crowd tagging along behind the Lord, he probably thought, "There's no reason to get fanatical about all this." So he replies to Jesus, "Lord...me first." He wanted to be around his home when his father died, so he could bury him. That's not a bad thing—it's just not putting Jesus first.

The third man also promised to follow Jesus, but he first wanted to go home and have a series of "farewells." Once again it was, "Lord, I will follow You, but let me first..." In other words, his plan was to follow Christ at some time in the future. Jesus said that "discipleship" needs to begin *now*!

Some people like the idea of being called a "disciple of Jesus Christ." But Jesus points out that it sometimes involves turning your back on "the good" in favor of "the best." When so-called followers of Christ take their hands off the plow, in order to look backwards at what they are leaving behind, they soon slow up and find a reason to go "back to the barn." If they are a true believer, they will still be a believer—they just won't be a disciple.

In the crowd following Jesus there were some true believers who were born again, but they just weren't willing to serve Jesus as first in their lives. How about You? Is Jesus *number one* in your life?

[See also: Matthew 8:19-22]

## WHAT DO YOU THINK?

1. What was Jesus beginning to concentrate on, even while He was training His disciples?

2. Isn't it a good thing that the man Jesus invited to be His disciple wanted to be there when his father died, so he could give him a proper burial?

3. Explain in your own words the meaning of Jesus' illustration of the farmer who started plowing his field and began to look backward instead of looking ahead.

## ANSWERS TO YOUR QUESTIONS

1. *Jesus was beginning to focus on the fact that He would soon be heading to Jerusalem where He would die on Calvary's cross.*

2. *It is a good thing, but it could also be an excuse for not wanting the sacrifice that comes with being one of Jesus' disciples. A disciple puts Jesus and His will first before everything else.*

3. *Personal opinion. PARENTS: It's important here to emphasize that a believer in Christ who "looks back" does not lose her salvation. She does, however, miss out on the joy and reward for being a disciple/servant of the Living God.*

*Everyone is my neighbor*

## 37. WHO IN THE WORLD IS MY NEIGHBOR?

*And behold, a certain lawyer stood up and put Him to the test, saying, "Teacher, what shall I do to inherit eternal life?"...But wishing to justify himself, he said to Jesus, "And who is my neighbor?"*

Luke 10:25, 29

When a lawyer, trying to trip up the Lord, asked Him, "Teacher, what shall I do to inherit eternal life?" he was given a surprising answer. Jesus told him that he needed to love God perfectly and also to love every person in the world (which would include even the most horrible criminal). That sounds a little different than Jesus' message to Nicodemus that unless he was *born again*, he would not go to heaven (John 3:16). Why the difference?

Jesus, being the Son of God, is able to look right into people's hearts and see the reasons why people say what they do. In the lawyer's case, I'm sure the Lord saw a proud man, convinced he deserved heaven, but was still determined to trap Jesus and make Him look foolish.

I believe the Lord Jesus was telling this proud lawyer that if he was perfect—like God is—he would not even need a savior. Because we are all lost sinners who primarily live for ourselves, no human could love God as Jesus described. On top of that, we all mainly live to please ourselves. Could any person say that he loves any other individual as much as himself? We usually love family and a few others with a stronger love, but do I love all people of the world as much as I love myself? I can't truthfully say I do.

Instead of humbling himself and turning to Christ in repentance, the lawyer tried to pin Jesus down and argue fine points like, "Who is my neighbor?" Who must I love like myself, and are there any exceptions? How about that strange family across the street?

So Jesus, as He did so often, told a simple story that even a child could understand—the parable of the Good Samaritan. As I read this wonderful story that Jesus told in order to explain to the lawyer and those who crowded around Him, who exactly qualifies as their neighbors, I have to ask myself, "Who is *my* neighbor?" and "Do I love everyone in the world as much as I love *me*?"

Would I be willing to show compassion and kindness to all people even in my own country to the same degree as I would want for myself? Am I actually burdened about the well-being of the Eskimos in the Arctic or the Zulu tribe in Africa—especially that they would come to know Jesus? In all honesty, I rarely even think of them. Do I think about my own well-being? All the time!

What was the Lord's message to this lawyer's question, "What shall I *do* to inherit eternal life?" I believe Jesus was saying something like, "Rather than asking Me what you should "do", you should be asking Me to forgive your sins, and to give you eternal life through faith in Me, the Son of God."

And who is your neighbor? Everyone!

## WHAT DO YOU THINK?

1. Do you think the lawyer asked Jesus about eternal life because he genuinely wanted to be saved or born again? Why or why not?

2. Who do you think would be able to fulfill the requirements for eternal life that Jesus gave to the lawyer? What was the point, then, of the Lord even saying that?

3. Loving your neighbor as much as you love yourself is obviously not the way to be saved. Do you think it's possible to love others as much as yourself? How could we ever do that?

―――∞―――

## ANSWERS TO YOUR QUESTIONS

1. *No. Luke says, "...a certain lawyer stood up and put Him to the test..." He obviously wanted to argue and make Jesus and His teaching look bad.*

2. *No one could love God perfectly all the time, nor could he love all people equal to the way he loves himself. I believe Jesus wanted to show the lawyer that there was nothing he could do to inherit eternal life. Like all of us, the lawyer needed to realize that he was a lost sinner and needed to trust in Jesus as his Savior.*

3. *Because we all have a sinful nature, we tend to first of all love ourselves. In order to love other people—including the unlovely—we all need the Lord Jesus in our hearts to love others. He is the One who loves all people of the world, and we need His love.*

*A neighbor cares for others*

## 38. IT TAKES A SAMARITAN

*"But a certain Samaritan, who was on a journey, came upon him [the injured man]; and when he saw him, he felt compassion, and came to him, and bandaged up his wounds..."*
*Luke 10:33, 34*

    Jesus had a wonderful way of using simple stories to teach important truths. In this story, it sounds at first like one man was kind to an injured man and two others were uncaring. But as with most of Jesus' parables and stories, when you dig down into them, there is so much more.

    During the Lord's time on earth, the Samaritans (people of Samaria) and the Jews were sworn enemies. The Jews looked down on those from Samaria (the area just to the north of Judea and Jerusalem), because they were part Jew and part Gentile—not purely from the nation of Israel.

    However, in this story, both the priest and the Levite (ancestor of Levi), looked the other way and ignored their injured countryman (let's call him Joshua). Not so the Samaritan—we'll give him the name Samuel. I believe the Lord's main point here was that *everyone in the world* is our neighbor, even if both of our countries don't get along. But there is more to see in the story by looking closer at the Samaritan and the injured man.

    Joshua could very well be a picture of all mankind—sinful, hurting, and lost without a savior. The bandits of course, are a picture of: the world, the flesh (our old natures), and the devil. How about the priest and the Levite? They seem to represent uncaring, unfeeling people of the world who look away when they see someone in need. They operated by the exact letter of the Law and not by the Holy Spirit.

    The Samaritan, Samuel, risked his own life in such a dangerous area, to stop and care for the injured Joshua. It's not difficult to see a vivid picture of the Savior Himself in the life of the Samaritan:

- Samuel was on a journey. Jesus left heaven to come to earth, to die for the sins of all mankind.

- He felt compassion for the injured man. Jesus has a heart of love for all people, and He suffered death on the cross so that we might live forever.
- Samuel came to the aid of the dying. All people are dead in trespasses and sin—Jesus is the only solution.
- He didn't just patch up Joshua, but provided for him in a permanent way. Jesus seeks us, finds us, and wants to heal us from our sin problem forever.
- Samuel had money to pay for the inn. Jesus paid our entire account before God the Father.
- He announced to the innkeeper that he was going to return to take care of anything that was still needed. Jesus promised to return one day when He will settle all accounts and make all things right.

What a wonderful lesson for all of us, that we would show mercy to those we meet in need, instead of crossing to the other side of the street.

# WHAT DO YOU THINK?

1. What was the relationship like between the Jews and the Samaritans? Why?

2. In Jesus' story, who did Joshua, the injured Jew, possibly represent or picture?

3. The Good Samaritan, who we called Samuel, paid Joshua's entire bill at the inn. What is that most likely picturing for us?

---

# ANSWERS TO YOUR QUESTIONS

1. *The Jews hated the Samaritans because they were "half-breeds." They were partly Jewish and partly Gentile. The Jews felt they were superior because they were God's chosen people. God never intended for them to hate other nations who weren't like them.*

2. *Joshua, the injured Jew, is a good picture of all the people of the world. Without faith in Christ, they are lost and hurting in their sin, with no hope of eternal life in heaven.*

3. *Jesus paid our entire "sin debt." When we trust in His death, burial, and resurrection, we become His born again child.*

*Why are you so uptight?*

## 39. MARTHA WAS ANXIOUS AND ANGRY

*But Martha was distracted with all her preparations; and she came up to Him [Jesus], and said, "Lord, do You not care that my sister has left me to do all the serving alone? Then tell her to help me."*
*Luke 10:40*

Can't you just picture dear Martha? She wants so badly to have a perfect meal for the perfect Son of God. It would make her feel so good to have Jesus lean away from the table, when He was finished, and say, "What a fantastic dinner! I don't know if I've ever had a more delicious meal."

In order to do that, all the hot dishes have to be ready at the same time; the cool water has to be drawn from the well; the best napkins and utensils have to be in place—everything has to be just "Martha-perfect."

She's thinking, "I could sure do with some help here. Look at my sister Mary—sitting there on the floor listening to Jesus like she had nothing else in the world to do. Can't she see that getting this great meal on the table right now is more than I can do by myself? How inconsiderate! See if I do anything special for her in the future. I'll just mention it right away to Jesus, with a few sighs and lots of emotion, of course, and He'll rebuke her for her selfishness. It's better that the Lord does it anyway. It will help her remember for the next time."

Two things that happen when we get anxious and angry are that we forget who God is, and we ignore what He has promised. When Martha's sighs get louder and louder, but still don't break up the Lord's conversation with Mary, Martha decides to take it to the next level. Today's verse says that, "she came up to Him [Jesus], and said, 'Lord, do you not care?'" When our minds are befuddled with bad attitudes, we don't even mind accusing Jesus Christ of "not caring." Normally Martha would never dream of accusing the Son of God of being uncaring. Surely she loved the Lord Jesus just like Mary did. But because her own plans for a perfect meal took first place over Christ's plans to encourage Mary, she just got more uptight and angry when things didn't work out the way she wanted.

Unfortunately things got worse for Martha, which usually happens when we stay anxious and angry. She began to give orders to the Son of God. I'm sure that once Martha got her heart right, she was shocked and embarrassed that she had actually ordered the Lord, "then tell her to help me."

Wow! That's kind of a scary situation when you think about it. Here was little old Martha ordering the Creator of the entire universe to do something she wanted. What is Jesus going to do? Will He strike her down with lightning or punish her with leprosy?

Stay tuned!

## WHAT DO YOU THINK?

1. Where did things first begin to go wrong for Martha?

2. What wrong attitudes clouded Martha's mind as she was preparing a meal for the Lord Jesus?

3. If we don't confess our anxiety and anger to the Lord as sin, it just builds and builds. What two extreme things did Martha do that showed she had not confessed her sin?

## ANSWERS TO YOUR QUESTIONS

1. *Personal opinion. PARENTS: A group discussion might work out well here.*

2. *Martha first went wrong when she made her own plans to really impress the Lord with a great meal, instead of finding out what the Lord's plans were. When things didn't work out quite like she wanted, she became anxious and angry.*

3. *First Martha asked the Lord, "...do You not care...?" Without even waiting for an answer, she ordered Jesus, "Then tell her to help me."*

*What is most important of all?*

## 40. ONLY ONE THING IS IMPORTANT

*And she had a sister called Mary, who moreover was listening to the Lord's word, seated at His feet... "but only a few things are necessary, really only one, for Mary has chosen the good part, which shall not be taken away from her."*
*Luke 10:39, 42*

Of course Jesus diagnosed Martha's problem accurately. After Martha questioned the Lord's caring spirit and then gave Him an order, He answered her kindly, "Martha, Martha, you are worried and bothered about *so many things*." So her problem was that she was "worried and bothered" about a lot of things in her life—probably more than just the dinner.

It could be that her finances were low and she wasn't sure how they could buy groceries the next week. It's possible too that she was worried about unexplainable pain in the area of her heart. Was she on the verge of a heart attack? And finally, how were they going to make their next mortgage payment, especially since she had just lost that extra house-cleaning job she had.

How could she have avoided becoming worried and bothered about "so many things"? To begin with, she could have sat down at Jesus' feet and poured out her worries to the only One who could do something about them. Forget the meal; the spiritual condition of her heart was far more important.

Even though the Lord could have been offended by Martha's tone and attitude, He was very gracious with her. He was honest to point out to her the reason for her worry, but He didn't leave her in that sorry state. Jesus went on to give her some amazing advice—and advice that applies to us as well.

You might want to underline verse forty-two in your Bible, and come back to it often. Here in a few words, Jesus gives us the answer to a life that is filled with "so many things" like school, friends, soccer practice, church youth group, music lessons, exams, and family. The Lord said, "But only a *few* things are necessary, really *only one*, for Mary has chosen the good part, which shall not be taken away from her."

That's a lot of good advice in a short sentence, isn't it? Jesus wanted Martha to understand that in all of life's challenges, there is one and only one priority and it overshadows all others. What is it? To love Jesus with all your heart, to obey His Word with His help, and to bring all of your worries to Him. The apostle Peter wrote, "...casting all your anxiety upon Him, because He cares for you" (1 Peter 5:7).

Jesus finished the conversation with Martha by pointing out that He was not going to ask Mary to get up and help Martha. Mary was doing the right thing—fellowshipping with the very Son of God. It didn't really matter if they didn't eat dinner until later on—or maybe not at all. Communion with the living Christ is "Number One"!

## WHAT DO YOU THINK?

1. What did Jesus say were Martha's two main problems as she prepared dinner for the group?

2. What should Martha have done instead of worrying and getting angry at both Mary and Jesus?

3. What was Mary doing right that Jesus said would not be taken away from her? How would that apply to us?

## ANSWERS TO YOUR QUESTIONS

1. *Jesus said that Martha was "worried" and "bothered" as she prepared the meal.*

2. *Martha should have sat down at Jesus' feet like Mary did, poured out her concerns to the Lord, including her worries, and asked Him to help her.*

3. *Jesus said that Mary was doing the one thing more important than any other—having fellowship with the Lord and learning from Him. We need to make it top priority in our own lives—developing a deep love relationship with our heavenly Father.*

*Jesus wants us to pray constantly*

## 41. WHEN IN DOUBT, KEEP ON PRAYING!

*And He said to them, "Suppose one of you shall have a friend, and shall go to him at midnight, and say to him, 'Friend, lend me three loaves;'... yet because of his persistence [repeatedly asking] he will get up and give him as much as he needs."*
*Luke 11:5, 8*

What a great story Jesus told to help His followers (and us) understand that we need to keep on asking God to supply our needs—even if He doesn't seem to answer right away.

A certain man (we'll call him Joseph) had a friend arrive at his house late at night, and he wanted to give the traveler a late supper. Not having any bread, he went to his neighbor to borrow some. The neighbor and his family were all in bed and didn't want to get up. The key point of the story was that Joseph kept knocking and asking because he wanted to provide for his friend. Finally, because of Joseph's persistence [not giving up], his neighbor got out of bed and gave him all the bread he needed.

Jesus was not teaching that He is reluctant to answer our prayers. It's just the opposite! We aren't His neighbors; we are His children. He just wants us to keep looking to Him patiently while waiting for Him to answer in His way and His time.

When my wife, Del, was first saved, at twenty-four years of age, we began to pray that all her family would be saved also. Over the years, many of her family have trusted in Jesus Christ for salvation, and we thank Him for working in their lives.

Del's dad was a very strong man—physically and emotionally. He had worked his way up from very poor beginnings in Detroit, to being a successful farmer and business owner. He felt he had made it on his own, through hard work and pinching his pennies. "Papa" was a self-made man, or so he thought.

Our family prayed for him for twenty-nine years, thinking all the time that every tribe and tongue would be reached with the Gospel before he would see his need for a savior. We were missionaries in Panama when we got the news that Papa had suffered a serious heart attack, and was in the intensive care unit of the hospital. I'm sure he wondered if he would ever leave there alive.

One afternoon, the pastor of our church visited Papa in his hospital room and shared with him a number of salvation Bible verses from the book of Romans. When the pastor finished reading, he said something like, "Frank, would you like to receive Jesus Christ as your Savior right now, and know for certain that you will go to heaven when you die?"

Papa answered, "I would!"

"Would you like to pray about it right now?"

Again, Papa said, "Yes, I would." And so, right there, this seventy-eight year old father and grandfather became a new child of God.

The next day, the pastor called us in Panama to share the good news with us. We had prayed for almost thirty years for "dear Papa" to receive Christ, and God had answered our prayers.

## WHAT DO YOU THINK?

1. The neighbor in Jesus' story did not want to get out of bed to answer his friend's request for some bread. Was the Lord teaching that God the Father is reluctant to answer prayer, but He will eventually answer if we ask enough times? What was He teaching?

2. How is the Christian's situation different from the man in Jesus' story who was asking his neighbor for bread?

3. Since prayer is not about twisting God's arm to give us what we want, what lesson is the Father most likely wanting to teach us—especially when He doesn't answer right away?

## ANSWERS TO YOUR QUESTIONS

1. *Throughout the Bible, God urges us to pray—to come to Him as often as we want and for as long as we want (See 1 Thessalonians 5:17). Jesus spent a lot of time praying when He was here on earth. God is not like a dispensing machine where we pray and out pops an answer. The Father is not reluctant to answer our prayers—He just wants us to learn that prayer is about God's will being done according to His own schedule.*

2. *In Jesus' story, the neighbor of the man asking to borrow bread was a friend, but he still put his own family first. He didn't want to wake them up. In our situation, God is our heavenly Father, and we are His eternal children. He loves us with a divine love.*

3. *I believe God wants to teach His children dependence on Him, regardless of circumstances, and total trust in the promises He made in His Word.*

*Jesus compares Himself to Jonah*

## 42. WHAT IS THE SIGN OF JONAH?

*And as the crowds were increasing, He began to say, "This generation is a wicked generation; it seeks for a sign, and yet no sign shall be given to it but the sign of Jonah."*
*Luke 11:29*

You would think that Jesus would be thrilled with the huge crowds that followed Him. Although the disciples probably were, Jesus was too discerning for that. As the Son of God, He knew exactly why every single person was there. Let's imagine one small group that might have been standing directly in front of Jesus one day:

- Simeon was a Pharisee, whose father and grandfather had been Pharisees also. He was sure Jesus was nothing more than a phony magician. He heard that this Nazarene claimed to heal the sick and raise the dead. Simeon was going to watch Him very carefully to try and expose how he did his "tricks."
- Tabitha was a rich widow who owned a huge home in the wealthy area of Jerusalem. She was bored with her life. And then she heard of this man from Galilee who could feed thousands of people with a few loaves and fishes. That would be entertaining.
- James, on the other hand, was a humble sheepherder from the hills of Judea. Only in his late teens, he heard the rabbi in the synagogue read from the Old Testament Scriptures that God would one day send His Son to earth. Could this Galilean carpenter possibly be the Messiah of Israel?

The hum of conversation throughout the crowd suddenly stopped with Jesus' stern rebuke about their wickedness. What did He mean that the only sign they would receive would be "the sign of Jonah"?

It's well worth reading the short Old Testament book named after the prophet Jonah. At first he resisted going to the city of Nineveh, even though God specifically commanded him, "Arise, go to Nineveh the great city, and cry against it, for their wickedness has come up before Me" (Jonah 1:2). But after a *whale* of a "three-day fish experience," God miraculously restored him to his world again and he followed through on God's plan for him. Jesus used the story of Jonah to teach the crowd that one day He would be killed, His body would be placed in a tomb for three days, and then He would rise from the grave alive.

Some of the people in the crowd following Jesus wanted to see Him perform miracle after miracle so they could judge His divine origin. They were unwilling to simply trust His word that He came from God.

Can you see how Jonah's three day experience inside a great fish was a picture or illustration of Jesus' death, burial, and resurrection? And what was the point of Jesus' statement? He was saying that He did not come to earth to perform miracles for the entertainment of people like the Pharisee Simeon and the rich woman Tabitha. He was telling them that He was in fact the Messiah of Israel—the hope of the sheepherder James. His purpose was to die for the sins of all mankind so He could forgive their sin and give them eternal life.

[See also: Matthew 12:38-42; Mark 8:11-12; John 2:18-25; 6:30]

## WHAT DO YOU THINK?

1. Why wasn't Jesus impressed with the large crowds that followed Him?

2. Some of the people followed Jesus for the wrong reasons. What could be some of those reasons?

3. What was the "sign of Jonah" that Jesus was talking about?

## ANSWERS TO YOUR QUESTIONS

1. *Jesus knew the heart and mind of every person in the crowd. He realized that a good number only followed Him for what they could personally get from Him, rather than repenting of their sins and trusting in Jesus as their Savior.*

2. *Those reasons could include:*
   - *Receiving food from a miracle like the loaves and fishes.*
   - *Being entertained by watching Jesus perform miracles.*
   - *Being healed of their illnesses.*
   - *Being curious*
   - *Waiting for Jesus to say something against the Roman government so they could report Him to the authorities.*
   - *Hoping Jesus might turn His miraculous powers against the cruel Romans.*

3. *Jesus told the crowd that He was not going to perform miracles (or give them a sign) just to prove to them that He actually was the Messiah of Israel. They had the Old Testament Scriptures which told the story of Jonah being three days in the belly of a great fish, and then being restored to his world. This was a picture or illustration of Jesus' future death, burial for three days, and His resurrection. The crowd needed to believe Jesus' words and not insist that He perform miracles for them.*

## 43. THE EYE—A TWO-WAY STREET

*"The lamp of your body is your eye; when your eye is clear, your whole body also is full of light; but when it is bad, your body also is full of darkness."*
Luke 11:34

Did you know there is such a thing as a "spiritual cataract"? When a person has a physical eye cataract, the lens in his eye becomes cloudy, and eventually he isn't able to see at all. In today's verse, Jesus is speaking to many who wanted to see a sign or miracle to prove that He was the Messiah. They were unwilling to trust Jesus—the Light of the World—so that He could flood their lives with His light. The spiritual cataracts were their hardened, proud hearts.

I watched a scientist being interviewed on TV yesterday, and the interviewer kept emphasizing what a genius this man was. He had "mapped" or figured out all the various units that make up DNA—the "software" in each of our cells that makes us who we are. Throughout the program, I heard what a brilliant thinker this scientist was—maybe even the smartest man alive. The very last question the host of the show asked was, "Do you believe in God?" Without any hesitation, the scientist responded, "No, I don't believe there is such a person as God. With evolution, there isn't any need for God."

I felt sad watching this so-called brilliant man, realizing that if he maintains his present condition with "spiritual cataracts," he will never experience the light of Jesus Christ flooding his life.

Let's look a little closer at Jesus' actual words to the crowd. Physically speaking, when our eyes are healthy, the light around us enters our eyes and sends electrical signals to our brains about all that's going on around us. When our eye is diseased, the light is interrupted until eventually we cannot see anything.

In John's gospel we hear Jesus saying, "I am the light of the world; he who follows Me shall not walk in the darkness, but shall have the light of life" (John 8:12). If our hearts are willing to believe God's Word—that He died and rose again to save us—Jesus Christ comes to live within us through the Holy Spirit. Our life is filled with His light. Psalm 119:130 explains clearly that, "The entrance and unfolding of Your words give light… (The Amplified Bible)."

So the eye is like a two-way street. As Christians, our lives are filled with Christ's light and that light can flow out of us toward others. Have you noticed that our eyes are like mirrors of what is going on in our hearts? Eyes can seem dark and even evil when they are reflecting the hardness of an unsaved heart. But when someone walks in obedience to Christ, it almost seems like kindness and compassion are visible in her eyes. Maybe it's just the beauty of Jesus Christ!

[See also: Matthew 6:22, 23]

## WHAT DO YOU THINK?

1. What is an eye cataract? What is a "spiritual cataract"?

2. Did the Jewish scribes and Pharisees of Jesus' day have "spiritual cataracts"? Why or why not?

3. What does it mean that the eye is like a two-way street?


## ANSWERS TO YOUR QUESTIONS

1. *In a regular eye cataract, the lens of the eye becomes cloudy so that light is unable to penetrate through it. That eye eventually becomes blind. A "spiritual cataract" is a hardened, proud heart that prevents the light of our glorious Savior from penetrating that person's mind and heart.*

2. *Yes, the scribes and Pharisees had "spiritual cataracts." Because they were the so-called religious experts of Israel, they were proud of their positions. They felt they knew the Old Testament better than the average Hebrew, and also felt they kept the Jewish Law more carefully—thus they were "better" people. They believed they had no use for Jesus.*

3. *The eye is like a mirror. The Bible says that both Jesus and His Word are light. When that light enters our hearts through our spiritual eyes, it changes us. If a person's heart is wicked, that darkness and evil seem to show through the eyes. Similarly, if God's light changes our hearts and we are saved, His joy and kindness seem to make our eyes sparkle.*

## 44. WHO WANTS A DIRTY CUP?

*But the Lord said to him, "Now you Pharisees clean the outside of the cup and of the platter; but inside of you, you are full of robbery and wickedness."*

*Luke 11:39*

Jesus did not hold back a bit when it came to exposing the phoniness of the religious leaders of His day. If the Pharisees were truly godly, like Simeon and Anna (Luke 2:25, 36) who waited patiently for the Messiah, they would have recognized that Jesus was the Son of God.

In today's verse, a Pharisee, who invited Jesus home for a meal, revealed his lack of understanding of truth. All he could think of was whether Jesus washed His hands before the meal, according to the laws of the Jewish religious leaders (Mark 7:2-4). It wasn't even part of the Laws that God gave Moses for Israel.

Jesus used this occasion to expose what was really in the hearts of these so-called religious experts. Here are some of the "rotten attitudes" that grew from the lives of the Pharisees and scribes (lawyers) who worried more about their appearance (the outside of the cup), than the condition of their souls (the inside).

- They were so fussy about tithing or offering one-tenth of all that they had, that they even tithed little herbs that they grew. One Bible teacher said, "They excelled in what could be seen by others, but were careless about what only God could see."[6]
- The Pharisees loved to parade around the temple and the marketplace in their religious robes so people would be sure to recognize them and give them honor.
- The lawyers or scribes would put all kinds of rules on the Jewish people, but not lift a finger to help them.
- People who lived in Old Testament times and were just like these religious leaders of the time Jesus was on earth, killed the prophets God sent to help the nation of Israel. Very soon, these very scribes and Pharisees would be killing Jesus, God's beloved Son.

- They were not true believers in God and His Son Jesus, and they made it difficult for those who wanted to come to Christ.

How do these words affect you and your life? Let's not be guilty of cleaning up our outward appearance, while we ignore the condition of our hearts.

[See also: Matthew 23:1-36; Mark 12:38-40]

## WHAT DO YOU THINK?

1. What was the issue of hand-washing all about, at the Pharisee's house? Where did that ceremonial law come from?

2. What was the point of Jesus' teaching regarding the inside and the outside of a cup? (Read 1 Samuel 16:7)

3. What was wrong with the way the scribes and Pharisees walked around the temple and the marketplace? Isn't it good to be recognized by others as being religious?

## ANSWERS TO YOUR QUESTIONS

*1. The Pharisee was "surprised" that Jesus didn't follow the ceremonial law of hand-washing before the meal. Laws like this were not given by God to Moses for the Jewish people, but were made up by people like the Pharisees who wanted to show others how "religious" they were.*

*2. Jesus wanted the Pharisee to understand that he was concerned about his outward appearance even while he ignored the pride, jealousy, and greed in his heart. When God was instructing Samuel about what to look for in a king for Israel, He said, "...for God sees not as man sees, for man looks at the outward appearance, but the Lord looks at the heart" (I Samuel 16:7).*

*3. Even while their hearts were filled with sin, the scribes and Pharisees made a point of dressing and appearing so that the average Jew would recognize their positions as religious leaders, and give them honor and praise.*

## 45. WHO ARE YOU CALLING A HYPOCRITE?

*...He began saying to His disciples first of all, "Beware of the leaven of the Pharisees, which is hypocrisy."*
Luke 12:1

We know who the Pharisees are, but what is *leaven*? This is just another word for the yeast that a baker mixes into his bread dough to make it rise light and fluffy. Only a small amount of yeast spreads through the dough and causes it to increase greatly in volume, just as sin (which may appear to be small in the beginning) spreads throughout a person's life until it takes over. Because of this similarity, "yeast" in the Bible almost always refers to sin or evil.

Jesus pulled no punches when He told the crowd following Him to "beware" of the Pharisees' sin and their corrupt teaching. There were probably lots of sins to choose from, but Jesus zeroed in on their *hypocrisy*. This word comes from the Greek language and means "to play a part—like an actor in a play."[7]

Actors in Greek plays wore masks that helped the audience know what type of person they were playing. Behind their mask, they were probably altogether different. The "bad guy" in the play could have been a wonderful person.

Let's return to those hypocritical Pharisees. Why was Jesus so hard on them? The Lord explains that their hearts were full of sin—greed, hatred, jealousy, and especially pride. And yet, because they belonged to a religious group they paraded around pretending they were the holy leaders of Israel. They were like actors wearing smiley religious masks that hid decaying, corrupt, impure people. Jesus saw right through these imposters, and because He *is* truth, He had to expose their evil lies.

One of the most harmful aspects of the hypocritical Pharisees is that they were lying to and deceiving many of the people of Israel. Not only were these religious phonies headed for hell themselves, but they were dragging others down with them. If they were so religious, they should have been rejoicing that the Messiah had come. Jesus had to warn the people to "beware" of them.

How does that apply to us today? One obvious way is that we can act one way on Sundays when we attend church or youth group—wearing our "church mask." Then when Monday comes, we put on our "school or work mask" and blend perfectly into the world with its godless culture. Both masks can be unreal and we can wear them to please (or fool) other people.

Let's ask the Lord to help us to be *real*. That way we're pleasing to Jesus and other people too.

[See also: Matthew 16:5-7; Mark 8:14, 15]

## WHAT DO YOU THINK?

1. What is "leaven" and how did Jesus use the word to describe the Pharisees?

2. Where does the word "hypocrisy" come from, and why were the Pharisees perfect examples of this attitude?

3. You are obviously not a Pharisee, but can you think of a time when you acted in a hypocritical way, remembering that the word means, "to play a part—like an actor in a play"?

## ANSWERS TO YOUR QUESTIONS

1. *"Leaven" is another word for "yeast." The Pharisees were full of a variety of sins that spread through their hearts and minds like yeast spreads through a lump of bread dough. Then the Pharisees taught their corrupt principles to unsuspecting people.*

2. *The word "hypocrisy" comes from the Greek culture where actors in plays would wear masks that represented the characters they were playing. Their real personality could have been totally different. The Pharisees acted on the outside like they were the holiest of all Jewish people, in order to receive the praise and honor of those around them. Inside they were corrupt and evil.*

3. *Personal opinion. PARENTS: Although this principle is extremely important, it needs to be handled delicately. The parent might even want to start by sharing an example from his or her own life.*

## 46. HOW MUCH ARE YOU WORTH?

*"Are not five sparrows sold for two cents? And yet not one of them is forgotten before God. Indeed, the very hairs of your head are all numbered. Do not fear; you are of more value than many sparrows."*

*Luke 12:6, 7*

In our previous devotional, we learned that Jesus called the Pharisees "hypocrites" because they were more concerned with what other people thought of them than what God thought.

Would we ever act that way? I'm embarrassed to say that as a high school and college student, I was not willing to stand up as a Christian and be known as His child. I was saved when I was around seven years of age, but as I became a teenager, I was afraid to be known as a Christian. It was my secret. I was afraid of people and their opinions. That really made me no different than the Pharisees—I was a hypocrite too.

Jesus knew that the day of His death on the cross was coming soon, and He was preparing His disciples for that day. He encouraged them first of all, by addressing them as "My friends," and then urged them not to live in fear of ungodly people—even those who would harm them for their Christian testimony. Jesus comforted them with the truth that He was far more powerful than those who could harm them.

Just in case the disciples were still not sure if they could wholeheartedly trust Jesus in every situation, the Lord told them two amazing facts:

- They could buy tiny sparrows for pennies and yet God, as the sparrows' creator, knew each individual bird and how they were doing. But God loves His children far more than the sparrow. Isn't God capable then of watching over those of us who have believed on His Son?
- Every single hair on our heads has a number in God's mind. In other words, with all the other things God has to do, He knows the sum total of our hairs. God is also able to know all that we do and think. He sees every danger that might be ahead of us, so He can protect us before we're hurt.

Every time we see a little group of sparrows picking up seeds on the ground, we should remember our heavenly Father's great love for us.

[See also: Matthew 10:28-31]

## WHAT DO YOU THINK?

1. In what way was the author a hypocrite when he was a teenager?

2. As Jesus got closer to the day of His crucifixion, He began to prepare His disciples for being on their own. What one thing did He urge them *not* to do?

3. Just in case the disciples still could not put their whole trust in Jesus, what two facts did He encourage them with concerning God?

## ANSWERS TO YOUR QUESTIONS

1. *The author was saved at age seven, but in high school and college, he failed to stand up as a Christian, but tried to blend in with the crowd of unbelievers. He was afraid of other people's opinions.*

2. *Jesus urged His disciples to not be fearful of men—either what negative things they said about the disciples, or what harm they might do to them. The Lord reminded them that He was more powerful than anyone or anything.*

3. *First, Jesus told them that God the Father was aware of every single sparrow that was only worth a few pennies. How much more did He care for them? Secondly, God knew every hair on their heads and even the total number. Of course He could take care of them in any situation.*

## 47. IS GOD FAIR?

*And someone in the crowd said to Him, "Teacher, tell my brother to divide the family inheritance with me." But He said to him, "Man, who appointed Me a judge or arbiter over you?" And He said to them, "Beware, and be on your guard against every form of greed;"*

*Luke 12:13-15*

Let's pretend that there is a family by the name of the Bakers. Mr. and Mrs. Baker have two children—Joshua, who is eleven and Megan who is nine.

Josh and Megan were having a problem keeping their bedrooms neat and "picked up," so Mr. Baker decided to discuss the problem at the dinner table one Saturday night. "I'll make a deal with you guys. If you make your beds and keep your bedrooms neat and clean all this next week, you can stay up an extra hour this Saturday night." They all agreed.

Josh and Megan both started out well. Monday morning, however, Josh didn't get up when he was first called. Being short on time, he just threw his covers up and kicked some clothes on the floor under his bed. Megan was determined to stay up later on Saturday, so she took the time to work on her room.

When Saturday morning came and mom inspected the rooms, Megan's room looked like a model home, but Josh's room…well, that's another story. He missed making his bed on Tuesday and Friday. His dirty clothes were either under his bed or on the floor of his closet.

The verdict was in; Megan got to stay up until 10:00 P.M., but Josh had to hit the sack at nine. Josh began to complain by saying, "That's not fair. I'm older than Megan, and I should be able to stay up too." Dad settled it quickly. "You both knew the rules, and Josh, you didn't keep your end of the agreement."

That was definitely the fair thing to do, wasn't it? What about God? Is He fair? If everyone should be treated exactly the same, then everyone should be allowed to go to heaven when they die. But we know from the Bible that isn't true. On the other hand, if God gave us what we "deserve," all mankind would go to hell after death. However God is gracious, meaning that He gives "believers" what they *don't deserve*—the free gift of eternal life. Some people actually believe that, since they say that God is fair, He wouldn't send some to heaven and others to hell. But, His Word, the Bible, says that the only ones who go to heaven are those who believe in Jesus—that He died on the cross to pay their sin debt.

No, God isn't "fair" as we may think of equality, but He is true and faithful to His Word.

## WHAT DO YOU THINK?

1. What arrangement did Mr. and Mrs. Baker have with Josh and Megan to help them make their beds every day and keep their rooms tidy?

2. If being "fair" means that everyone should get the same things all the time, regardless of their behavior, was Mr. Baker being fair?

3. According to the definition of "fairness" in number two, is God fair? On what basis does God deal with men, women, and children? What's a good example of how God treats people differently?

---

## ANSWERS TO YOUR QUESTIONS

1. *The Bakers agreed that if Josh and Megan made their beds and kept their rooms tidy all that week, they could stay up an extra hour on Saturday night.*

2. *If "fair" means everyone always gets the same thing, then Mr. Baker was not fair. But Josh did not keep his end of the bargain, so he did not deserve a reward. Megan did what they all agreed to.*

3. *God would not follow the definition of "fairness" in number two either. Since we are all sinners, we all deserve hell. But because God is gracious, He provided a way to go to heaven—believing in Christ's death on the cross. Only those who believe in Him will go to heaven when they die.*

*Don't worry about your next meal!*

## 48. GOD PROMISES TO PROVIDE FOR US

*"And do not seek what you shall eat, and what you shall drink, and do not keep worrying. For all these things the nations of the world eagerly seek; but your Father knows that you need these things. But seek for His kingdom, and these things shall be added to you."*
Luke 12:29-31

There are two phrases in today's verses that, if followed by Christians, would totally change our thinking and our attitudes.

The first is, "Do not keep worrying." The Lord Jesus is trying to comfort both His disciples and Christians too, that because He is our Father, He promises to provide all our *needs*—although not all our *wants*. He even gives examples of how He feeds and clothes all of creation with His bounty. Why then wouldn't He provide for those for whom He died on Calvary's cross?

The second phrase is, "But your Father knows that you need these things." Don't you find a great deal of comfort in knowing that Jesus is aware of everything we need to live and serve Him? I'm sure He knows even better than we do ourselves.

Before our family could become missionaries, I had to quit my job as a veterinarian, in order for us to enter missionary training. After our yard sale, we had our car, our 4x8 trailer with all our belongings, and six hundred dollars. Our small home church promised to send us ten dollars each month to help us with our expenses. We were about to learn what "living by faith" means.

We began life at the New Tribes Mission (Canada) training school, and gradually our six hundred dollars became four hundred, then three hundred. We were sure that God led me to quit my job, and for us to go as a family into NTM. But where would the money come from for us to live the rest of our lives?

When we were down to about two hundred dollars, we received a letter from a widow in Saginaw, MI whom we barely knew. She said that she and her children wanted to adopt us as "their missionaries," and they began to send us a check every month. Soon another elderly lady, whom we had never met, wrote and said she wanted to support us regularly also.

God has continued faithfully over the past forty-two years, to meet all our needs that same way. And He keeps encouraging us with His words: "Do not keep worrying" and "Your Father knows that you need these things."

## WHAT DO YOU THINK?

1. In our devotional we talked about what Jesus told His disciples (and all Christians too), to encourage them that their heavenly Father takes responsibility for their needs. What are those two short phrases?

2. Can you think of some area that you have worried about recently?

3. Read Philippians 4:19. Explain this promise from God in your own words.

## ANSWERS TO YOUR QUESTIONS

1. *The two phrases of Jesus that we discussed are: "Do not keep worrying" and "Your Father knows that you need these things."*

2. *Personal opinion.*

3. *Personal opinion.*

*Jesus knew He had to die*

## 49. HE SET HIS FACE TO GO TO JERUSALEM

*And He was passing through from one city and village to another, teaching, and proceeding on His way to Jerusalem.*
*Luke 13:22*

Why was Jesus so determined to go to Jerusalem? Was it because He grew up in the small town of Nazareth, and wanted to visit the big city with all that it offered?

Before the Son of God even came to earth and was born in Bethlehem, He was heading for Jerusalem. After all, this was the city where many of God's prophets of the Old Testament were killed. And now, God the Father was sending His precious Son to bring salvation to the nation of Israel and the world. Would Israel recognize that this carpenter from Nazareth, who walked on water, healed the lame, and fed thousands from a young lad's lunch, was in fact their Messiah? The Jews were expecting a king—yes, the King of the Jews—and who did this poor Nazarene think He was, posing as the Hebrew monarch?

Jesus began His ministry in His home town, but the townspeople rejected Him—even wanted to kill Him. To them He was just Joseph the carpenter's son.

The Lord Jesus began to preach the kingdom of God in the towns and cities beyond Nazareth. But all the time, He was focused on Jerusalem—because that's where the shepherd was going to have to lay down His life for His sheep.

Earlier in His gospel Luke wrote, "And it came about, when the days were approaching for His ascension [return to heaven], that He resolutely [firmly] set His face to go to Jerusalem" (Luke 9:51).

I wonder how Jesus felt in His heart about heading to this great Jewish city. Was He excited? Was He fearful? Does the Bible have any clues as to what the Lord was thinking?

Hebrews 12:2 is one of the clearest: "…fixing our eyes on Jesus, the author and perfecter [completer] of faith, who for the *joy* set before Him, endured the cross, despising the shame…" Jesus was joyful because many would be forgiven of their sins by His going to the cross. He "endured" or put up with the cross because it was the only way for people to be saved. Finally, He "despised" the shame of hanging almost naked on a cruel Roman cross while the world watched Him die.

Doesn't it make you love Jesus all the more to realize that, knowing the shame and agony He was going to face in Jerusalem, He still set His face to go there?

## WHAT DO YOU THINK?

1. John 1:11 says, "He came to His own, and those who were His own did not receive Him." What does this verse mean?

2. What does it mean that Jesus "set His face" to go to Jerusalem?

3. Read Matthew 26:36-39. Can you explain these verses in your own words?

## ANSWERS TO YOUR QUESTIONS

1. *Jesus, God's Son, came to earth first as the Messiah of Israel—as their king and their Savior. But the majority of Jews—especially the religious leaders like the scribes and Pharisees—refused to accept Him as their king. They liked to see His miracles, but didn't want Him to be their God.*

2. *The Lord Jesus knew before He left heaven, that His purpose in coming to earth was to die for the sins of all mankind. For the three years of His actual ministry, He knew He would finally go to Jerusalem where He would be crucified. Jesus refused to be distracted from His heavenly purpose.*

3. *Personal opinion. It might be profitable to have all the family contribute their ideas.*

*The narrow door to salvation*

## 50. WHY ALL PEOPLE DON'T GET SAVED—CHOICE

*And someone said to Him, "Lord, are there just a few who are being saved?" And He said to them, "Strive [labor] to enter by the narrow door; for many, I tell you, will seek to enter and will not be able."*

Luke 13:23, 24

I think we would all agree that throughout biblical history, the majority of people did not obey God's commandments in the Old Testament, or receive Jesus Christ as their Savior in the New Testament. Since the Lord died on Calvary's cross two thousand years ago, that has continued to be the case. Among the crowds of people who hear God's truth, only a few choose to receive it for themselves.

When Jesus was asked if only a few were being saved, He answered that one reason was that the doorway to salvation was "narrow." Does that mean that God purposely made the opening to eternal life tiny so that only a minimal number of people could squeeze through?

No, that is not God's way. He opens His arms to the whole world. Just think about John 3:16 which many of us memorized as children. It begins with, "For God so loved the world, that He gave His only begotten Son…"

Well, if God made the way to salvation wide, why did Jesus say in this verse that the door is "narrow"?

Even though Jesus declared that salvation is a *free gift,* so many people want to earn or pay for salvation. So often when I ask a person if they will go to heaven when they die, they say, "Yes. Because I've done more good things in my life than bad, God should let me into heaven." They still felt they were good enough to deserve heaven, even after I read a verse to them like Ephesians 2:8, "For by grace [a gift] you have been saved through faith; and that not of yourselves, it is the *gift* of God…"

It's hard for us to admit that we are lost sinners, isn't it? We all tend to feel that we have quite a bit of "good" in us. But Jesus disagrees. He says that the way of salvation is narrow!

[See also: Matthew 7:13, 21-23; 8:11, 12]

## WHAT DO YOU THINK?

1. How does John 3:16 prove to us that God did not purposely make the door of salvation narrow?

2. Why do so many people believe that they don't need to accept God's offer of His free gift of salvation?

3. Explain this part of Ephesians 2:8, "For by grace [a gift] you have been saved through faith…"

## ANSWERS TO YOUR QUESTIONS

1. *Jesus said in John 3:16 that because God loves the world (or all people in it), He sent His Son to earth to die on the cross to pay their "sin debt." 2 Peter 3:9 says that God is not willing that any should perish (or die and go to hell), but that all should come to repentance.*

2. *So many people believe that they have done enough good in their lives that they deserve heaven. You cannot deserve heaven and accept God's free gift at the same time.*

3. *Personal opinion. To receive God's grace means to accept something good "for free," even though you deserve punishment. Salvation is a free gift that cannot be paid back. It can only be received by faith or trust.*

*Pride leads to delaying*

## 51. WHY ALL PEOPLE DON'T GET SAVED—PRIDE

*"Once the head of the house gets up and shuts the door, and you begin to stand outside and knock on the door, saying, 'Lord, open up to us!' then He will answer and say to you, 'I do not know where you are from... depart from Me, all you evildoers.'"*
*Luke 13:25, 27*

Jesus was a masterful story-teller. His stories almost always contained important truths about Himself, and about the need for the nation of Israel to repent of their sin and turn to Him.

The majority of Jewish people put off making a decision to believe Jesus' teaching. The Lord wanted them to understand that they would not always have the same access to Him that they presently did. Why did they procrastinate (delay making a decision)? The Israelite nation wrongly believed that because Jesus walked the streets of their cities and performed miracles, that they had a sure ticket into the kingdom of God.

As a back-up, the Jewish people knew they were descendants of Abraham, Isaac, and Jacob (called the Jewish "patriarchs" or fathers of the Jewish nation). Why wouldn't God take that into consideration and give them a "free pass" into the kingdom?

In today's verses, Jesus told a story about a man who prepared a banquet. The Lord compared Israel to people knocking at the man's door (the kingdom), but not being allowed to enter. Their pride and their procrastination kept them from being welcomed in.

One thing Jesus said in His parable that would have been particularly offensive to the Jews, was that "Gentiles" (or non-Jews, who were looked at as being like dogs) would come from all around the world at the end of time, and be welcomed into Christ's kingdom, while the majority of Jews would be turned away at the door.

Can we see ourselves in Jesus' parable? Many people respond in a very similar way when I ask them if they are "born again." Their answer might be, "Well, I'm a _____ (some type of church or denomination)" as if that is a ticket to heaven. Others say, "I grew up in a Christian home." God might say to them the same thing He said to the people in today's verses: "I do not know where you are from."

Let's not be guilty of putting off making a decision to receive Jesus Christ as our Savior like the people in Jesus' story.

## WHAT DO YOU THINK?

1. What two reasons were mentioned in today's devotional for why the Jewish people procrastinated or delayed in preparing properly for entrance into God's kingdom?

2. What would have been especially insulting to the Jews when Jesus mentioned that the door to His kingdom would have been closed to most of them?

3. In what way can we act like the Jews in Jesus' story?

## ANSWERS TO YOUR QUESTIONS

1. *Jesus had taught and done miracles in their cities, so it appeared like He favored the nation of Israel. A further reason for their delay was that as Jews, they were direct descendants of Abraham, Isaac, and Jacob, who were blessed by God.*

2. *The thought of some Jews being turned away from Christ's kingdom, while Gentiles from around the world were welcomed would have been extremely hard for the Jews to accept.*

3. *We can act like the Jews in Christ's parable if we procrastinate in making a decision to accept His free gift of salvation. Also, if we feel that God will accept us into heaven because we attend a particular church or grew up in a Christian home, we will not be allowed into heaven.*

*Jesus longs for people's salvation*

## 52. WHY ALL PEOPLE DON'T GET SAVED— STUBBORNNESS

*"O Jerusalem, Jerusalem, the city that kills the prophets and stones those sent to her! How often I wanted to gather your children together, just as a hen gathers her brood under her wings, and you would not have it!"*

*Luke 13:34*

One of my all-time favorite movies is called *The March of the Penguins*. I learned so much about the life of a community of these odd birds that can't fly. The filming in Antarctica was awesome! How the team was able to capture such detail in the penguins' yearly cycle boggles my mind.

One scene in particular has stayed with me. After the female lays one large egg, she leaves the egg with the male, and along with all the other females, begins the long trek to the sea. There, the females feast on fish for weeks. At some point they all head for home, much fatter and ready to feed their new offspring.

While the females are gone, the males all huddle together, each one holding their one egg on their feet so the frigid ice does not kill the developing baby. Then the male lowers his body over the egg so that his body heat provides the perfect temperature for the life within the egg to develop.[8]

In today's verse, Jesus uses the illustration of a mother hen. When the female chicken senses danger, she calls her little chicks to her. She fluffs her feathers and squats down so her babies can hide under her body and her wings (Psalm 91:4).

What a clear picture Jesus drew to describe the love He has in His heart for the Jewish people. He focuses here on the great city of Jerusalem that represented the nation of Israel. How He wanted them to receive Him as their king and their Savior, but for the most part, they refused. Some would welcome Him into the city with their "Hosannas!" but these same ones would later shout "Crucify Him!"

This chapter in Luke gives us at least three reasons why the majority of people do not get saved—they are not willing to take the *narrow way* of God's gift without works; they are proud and delay making a life-decision; and they stubbornly refuse to accept Jesus' offer.

Luke 19:41 says, "And when He approached [Jerusalem], He saw the city and wept over it..." How Jesus loves people and wants them to trust Him as their Savior! What a privilege to be able to call Him "Father"!

[See also: Matthew 23:37-39]

## WHAT DO YOU THINK?

1. What does today's verse say that Jesus wanted to do with the citizens of Jerusalem?

2. Describe in your own words the illustration Jesus used to describe His love for the Jewish people, represented by the city of Jerusalem (See Psalm 91:4).

3. Today's verse gives the third reason why not many people get saved. What is it?

## ANSWERS TO YOUR QUESTIONS

*1. Jesus wanted the people of Jerusalem to accept His words by faith and recognize Him as their Messiah and Savior.*

*2. Personal opinion.*

*3. After Jesus said that He wanted to gather the Jewish people to Himself, He said that the majority didn't want Him—they stubbornly refused to accept Him as their Messiah.*

*Humility is putting yourself last*

## 53. WHERE ARE YOU SITTING AT THE TABLE?

*"For everyone who exalts himself shall be humbled, and he who humbles himself shall be exalted."*
*Luke 14:11*

The TV program *American Idol* is very popular as I write this. Dozens of contestants start out at the beginning, hoping to sing their way to stardom. They all have one goal—to be famous and rich.

Various young singers are interviewed as the program continues week after week. One says, "I just have to win—this is my big break and I want to go to Hollywood or Las Vegas to perform." Others say, "I just want to be a star!"

In today's verse, Jesus was eating at the house of a leader of the Pharisees on the Sabbath (Saturday). He noticed that the other guests were trying to sit in the most honored seats at the table, probably as close to the host as possible. Why do you think the guests were doing that? The food wasn't any tastier there.

I think they wanted to impress the other guests at the table that they were "important people." They longed to be "famous." We love to impress other people, don't we? We all want to be "first in line."

In reality, Jesus is the only One who deserves to be impressed. All our actions and words should be for His glory rather than our own. In other words, life is not primarily about us being famous, but about the Lord receiving honor in all that we do.

Jesus said, "Every one who exalts himself shall be humbled." If a person's goal is only that they can be famous, that they can be a star, and that others will give them "box seats" at important events, sooner or later they are going to be disappointed and fall from self-made stardom. The Lord Himself—the creator of all the heavens—calls Himself "gentle and humble in heart" (Matthew 11:29).

The next time you hear a person say something like, "This is my big chance to be famous," just remember Jesus also said, "…and he who humbles himself shall be exalted" (Luke 14:11).

Wouldn't you rather have the Lord honor you than to exalt yourself?

[See also: Matthew 23:12; James 4:6]

## WHAT DO YOU THINK?

1. What are your thoughts about a person wanting to be famous or a "star"?

2. What did Jesus notice at the dinner that caused Him to teach on "humility"?

3. Why do people usually want the best seats or to be first in line? Whose glory are they seeking? Whose glory should be of primary concern?

## ANSWERS TO YOUR QUESTIONS

1. *Personal opinion. You may want to ask each child.*

2. *Jesus noticed that the other guests were trying to get the best seats at the dinner table or the places of honor. These seats were probably the closest to the host who was a leader of the Pharisees.*

3. *We love to impress other people, and we also want the very best available for ourselves. These choices are obviously for our own benefit and pleasure. The apostle Paul wrote, "Whether, then, you eat or drink or whatever you do, do all to the glory of God" (I Corinthians 10:31).*

*What did Jesus mean by "hate"?*

## 54. SHOULD WE HATE OUR OWN FAMILY?

*Now great multitudes were going along with Him; and He turned and said to them, "If anyone comes to Me, and does not hate his own father and mother and wife and children and brothers and sisters, yes, and even his own life, he cannot be My disciple."*
*Luke 14:25, 26*

Let's consider what these puzzling verses *don't* mean, and then what they *do*.

The best way to understand what a particular verse means is to compare it with other similar Bible verses. Since we know that Scripture does not contradict itself (or say opposite things), we know that Jesus cannot be telling the crowd that they should be holding bitter, angry, hostile feelings against their own family members.

Husbands are urged to *love* their wives (Ephesians 5:25). Jesus told the Apostles, "A new commandment I give to you, that you love one another, even as I have loved you, that you also love one another" (John 13:34). Finally, in Titus 2:4, the apostle Paul wrote, "that they may encourage the young women to love their husbands, to love their children…"

So what did Jesus mean when He talked to the people about *hating* their own family members? [PARENTS: This might be an appropriate point to stop and get your children's thoughts on this question.] We read in today's verses that great multitudes were following Jesus. Since He could read each person's heart, He knew that many in the crowd only wanted to see miracles done or maybe even get some free food. Jesus wanted the people of Israel to repent of their sins and believe His message—not just be entertained. If He had only wanted a huge number of followers, He could have done more miracles, but He really wanted believers who would also be "disciples."

So Jesus challenged the crowd with what it means to be a true follower or learner of Christ. One Bible teacher said it so well: "*Salvation* is open to all who will come by faith, while *discipleship* is for believers willing to pay the price."[9]

When Jesus used the word "hate" here, He didn't mean "bitter, angry attitudes," but rather a "less intense love" (See Genesis 29:30). Our love for the Lord must be so strong and intense that our love for others, including family and ourselves, is a distant second.

I'm sure when Jesus finished, the crowd thinned out considerably. How about you? Are you willing to pay the cost of being Jesus' disciple?

[See also: Matthew 10:37-39]

## WHAT DO YOU THINK?

1. Why do you think Jesus made the challenging statement in today's verses to the huge crowd following Him?

2. Was Jesus telling the crowd that they had to have bitter, angry feelings toward their families and themselves in order to be His disciples?

3. What is the cost to being a disciple of Jesus? What did our salvation cost Him?

## ANSWERS TO YOUR QUESTIONS

1. *Jesus undoubtedly made that statement because He realized the crowd was following Him for the wrong reasons. He wanted to be honest with them so they understood what being a true follower of Jesus Christ involves.*

2. *Jesus was not saying that His disciples should have bitter, angry feelings toward others, since we read other verses that say we should love our family members. He was talking about the degree or amount of love—it should be so much more intense for the Lord than for others, including ourselves.*

3. *The cost of discipleship is that we love the Lord Jesus far more than others (including family and ourselves). Our salvation meant Jesus dying on the cross, so it cost Him everything.*

*The importance of planning.*

## 55. WHEN A PLAN COMES TOGETHER

*"For which one of you, when he wants to build a tower, does not first sit down and calculate the cost, to see if he has enough to complete it?"*
                              Luke 14:28

Years ago there was a TV adventure series called *The A-Team*. The team members were all experts in something, and when they brought a criminal to justice, their leader would say, "I love it when a plan comes together!"[10]

When Jesus told a story of a man building a tower, He was describing the "cost of discipleship." At the same time, He was teaching the importance of *planning* in your life, rather than just *reacting* "on the spur of the moment."

You may be thinking that you are too young to worry about planning activities in your life. Or maybe you think that because of your age, others do all the planning for you. Here are several areas you may want to prayerfully think about:

- Do you have a plan for reading your Bible on your own? How about trying to read it through from Genesis to Revelation in one year—or even in two years?
- Is there a special person in your life like an uncle, a cousin, or a friend, who isn't saved? Why not develop a plan to pray daily for their salvation? My wife and I prayed for a close relative for 29 years. When he was seventy-eight years of age and in the hospital with a heart attack, he trusted Christ as his Savior.
- You probably earn some money from allowance or odd jobs. Besides giving a portion of it to the Lord every week, why don't you save for a mission trip with your youth group some day—to the Ukraine, Portugal, or Nicaragua?
- Is there a musical instrument you would like to learn to play? Without a plan to practice regularly and to keep improving, you aren't going to get there. Wouldn't it be great to have that skill when you are an adult?

- Jesus was teaching the crowd following Him that you need to make a plan to be His faithful disciple—it doesn't just happen automatically. You need to plan that whatever Jesus' will is for you, you will do it—whatever the cost, you will pay it.

If you become a "planner" around God's will, your life will become a lot more orderly, and best of all, you will please and glorify your Savior, Jesus Christ.

## WHAT DO YOU THINK?

1. What principle of life was Jesus teaching in this verse that relates to being His disciple?

2. Can you think of an area in your life where you actually sat down and wrote up a plan—in your journal or diary? If you have, what are your thoughts about doing that? PARENTS: You might want to ask each child of suitable age this question. You also might want to set them up with a journal, and help them become a recorder and planner, until it becomes a habit.

3. If you begin to be a planner around God's will, what are two likely positive results?

## ANSWERS TO YOUR QUESTIONS

1. *Jesus was teaching that a wise person will sit down and make a plan before undertaking an important project—especially about being Christ's faithful disciple.*

2. *Personal opinion.*

3. *If you become a planner around God's will, your life will become a lot more orderly, and best of all, you will please and glorify your Savior Jesus Christ.*

*What good is salt without flavor?*

## 56. SALT IS GOOD—AT TIMES

*"Therefore, salt is good; but if even salt has become tasteless, with what will it be seasoned? It is useless either for the soil or for the manure pile; it is thrown out."*
*Luke 14:34, 35*

Can you imagine how *blah* our world would be without ordinary salt? Picture a pizza with no salt in it at all—it would taste like the cardboard box it came in.

As Jesus winds up His teaching on what it means to be His disciple, He compares His faithful "learners" to salt. Earlier, Jesus said to the Twelve on one of their mountain retreats, "You are the salt of the earth..." (Matthew 5:13). Why compare a faithful follower to a white crystal commonly found on our dinner tables?

Salt is a generous gift from God and is found throughout the world. Here are a few facts that you might find interesting:

- Salt (sodium chloride) is found in most of our body fluids and organs. Have you ever tasted how salty your tears are? We would soon die without this precious substance in exactly the right proportions. When we are seriously ill in the hospital, one of the first things a doctor will recommend is saline or salt water given intravenously.
- Sometimes salt is mined out of the ground. Other times it is close to the earth's surface, like the Bonneville Salt Flats in Utah and the Dead Sea in the Middle East.
- Salt is so important to our diet, that soldiers in Jesus' day received part of their salary in salt.
- It is a preservative. Before freezers and refrigerators, meat was packed in barrels of salt to keep it from decaying.
- Salt is an antiseptic that is often used to kill infections on the skin. Whenever I feel a sore throat coming on, I gargle with salt and warm water.

Why then did Jesus compare His faithful disciples to salt? Where there are several believers in a group of people, you will often notice that they will positively influence the group—with kindness, generosity, and a testimony of God's greatness.

However, if those same believers decide to turn their backs on the Lord and be just like the sinful unbelievers around them, what good are they? How can they possibly point people to Jesus Christ—they have "lost their flavor."

Notice the verse in Matthew 5:13 which says that if salt has lost its flavor (a disciple's Christian influence) it is "thrown out and trampled under foot by men." God will never throw His rebellious children away, but when we claim to be a Christian and lie, cheat, and steal, men will want nothing to do with us. They think, "If that's Christianity, I don't need it!"

Let's prayerfully determine that by God's strength, we're going to be "the salt of the earth" for His pleasure.

[See also: Matthew 5:13; Mark 9:50]

## WHAT DO YOU THINK?

1. Where is salt found in our bodies?

2. What did Jesus mean when He told His disciples they were "the salt of the earth"?

3. What happens when Jesus' disciples, like salt that has lost its "saltiness," turn away from Him and begin to act like sinful unbelievers?

## ANSWERS TO YOUR QUESTIONS

1. *Salt is found in almost all our body fluids and organs.*

2. *Salt adds a good flavor to food (like French fries). A true follower of Jesus adds a positive influence or "flavor" to whatever group of people he is with, by being kind, loving, caring, friendly, and honest.*

3. *Today's verses say that when salt becomes "tasteless," men (not God) throw it out because it is no longer useful or beneficial. When a disciple of Jesus ceases to walk in obedience to her Master, and commits the same sins as unbelievers, people will often reject her. They see her as a hypocrite, because she claims to be a Christian, and yet she acts like an unbeliever.*

*God never quits searching*

## 57. "UNTIL" IS DIFFERENT THAN "IF"

*And He told them this parable, saying, "What man among you, if he has a hundred sheep and has lost one of them, does not leave the ninety-nine in the open pasture, and go after the one which is lost, until he finds it?"*

*Luke 15:3, 4*

This is one of my favorite passages in the entire Bible. For one thing, it is a beautiful picture of a shepherd's love for every one of his sheep, but it also shows Jesus' attitude of loving concern toward us, His children.

Let's look down inside this story, where the beauty of this shepherd-sheep relationship blossoms. Picture a man who owns a hundred sheep, and he is out with his flock on a mountain pasture, along with his two sons, where the sun and rain have nourished the lush grass.

It's morning, and after a steaming cup of coffee to chase away the chill and dampness, he decides to count his sheep. When he arrives at the last ewe, he is only at ninety-nine. He must have counted wrong, so he goes over the flock again—still ninety-nine! And sure enough, it's the year-old lamb he calls "Daisy" that is missing.

During the night, Daisy must have gone exploring, and before long couldn't find her way back in the dark, to the security of the flock.

The shepherd's heart freezes at the thought of Daisy being all alone, because he loves her. Yes, she has a tendency to wander off, but she is "his lamb." He still remembers the day she was born. And there is so much danger out there.

The shepherd wastes no time in giving his two sons instructions regarding the ninety-nine, and then he takes off searching. For two days he searches the mountains for Daisy knowing he will never give up. He won't set a time and then return to the others—"if" he finds her. Verse four says "until" he finds it. That one word makes all the difference in the world.

We who know Jesus as our Savior are the sheep of God's flock. There may be a time when we wander away from our Father and

Shepherd, and are caught up in sin and rebellion. Jesus will go after us because we belong to Him. The Holy Spirit will work in our hearts as long as we're alive, to bring us back into that love relationship with our Shepherd, Jesus.

I don't know about you, but I sure like the phrase *"until"* He finds me, better than *"if"* He finds me.

[See also: Matthew 18:12-14]

## WHAT DO YOU THINK?

1. Does the shepherd decide ahead of time that he's only going to spend a certain amount of time hunting for his lost sheep?

2. What one word tells us that the shepherd (Jesus) will never give up trying to bring us back into His protective fold, when we Christians wander away from Him?

3. What thoughts do you have personally about the fact that if we who know Jesus wander away from Him, He will keep after us *until* He brings us back to Himself?

## ANSWERS TO YOUR QUESTIONS

1. *No, definitely not.*

2. *The one word is "until." That means that the heart of the Great Shepherd (Jesus) will never give up trying to bring us back into a deep love relationship with Himself. If believers become rebellious and cease to follow the Lord, He will never abandon us, but will keep working in our hearts.*

3. *Personal opinion.*

*Celebrating the wanderer's return*

## 58. CELEBRATE WITH ME!

*"And when he has found it, he lays it [his lost sheep] on his shoulders, rejoicing. And when he comes home, he calls together his friends and his neighbors, saying to them, 'Rejoice with me, for I have found my sheep which was lost!'"*
*Luke 15:5, 6*

If you ever had a thought that Jesus doesn't love His children, or "falls out of love" for them when they sin, these verses ought to be a great comfort to you. In the previous devotional, we saw how the Lord Jesus will pursue us when we wander away from Him, "until He finds us." Now, we see His joy and celebration when He finally draws us back to Himself—or, in other words, we quit being stubborn and rebellious, and turn away from our sin to His love.

In light of Jesus' parable, can't you just see Him finally spotting us, stuck in a rocky crevice? We're wet and cold, and we can't stop shivering. We've just about given up when we see His light swinging back and forth on the path as He searches for us.

And then He spots us! Let me first tell you what He doesn't do. He doesn't start ranting in a fit of anger, telling us what a horrible sheep we are—probably the worst in the flock. He also doesn't tell us how tired He is from two days of searching. Look again at today's verses and see the love pouring out of our Great Shepherd's heart. "And *when* He has found it, He lays it [the sheep] on His shoulders *rejoicing*." Did you notice that it says, "And *when* he has found it"? Isn't that thrilling? The Shepherd is overcome with joy because He has found His wayward sheep. He doesn't scoot the sheep back down the path—He carries it in His arms.

I've heard some people say that it was the custom of Jesus' day for the shepherd to purposely break the sheep's leg to keep it from wandering away again. I don't see any sign of that thinking in Jesus' story here at all. It's all rejoicing on the part of the shepherd.

What does he do then? Does he sneak the sheep back into the sheep fold as quietly as he can, so that no one notices? Is he embarrassed? He obviously is not pleased that his sheep has wandered away, but he calls all his friends together so they can celebrate and share in his joy.

That's just the way Jesus is when we wander away from Him and deny Him with our rebellion. When we come to our senses and repent of our sin, there He is. He's ready to put us on His shoulders, rejoicing. Have you ever seen such grace?

## WHAT DO YOU THINK?

1. In this particular parable told by Jesus, who does the one lost sheep represent?

2. Why do you think the shepherd in the story is so determined to find his sheep, and doesn't give up until he finally locates it? What does it tell you about our Great Shepherd, Jesus, and His heart?

3. Does the shepherd quietly sneak the wandering sheep back into the fold so that no one sees him? Is he embarrassed by his sheep's behavior?

## ANSWERS TO YOUR QUESTIONS

1. *The one lost sheep represents a Christian believer who chooses to walk away from fellowship with Jesus Christ. NOTE: Some feel the sheep is an unbeliever who is lost in sin and gets saved. The sheep in this parable belongs to the shepherd; is a part of the fold; and the shepherd says, "Rejoice with me for I have found MY SHEEP which was lost [wandered away]". See John 10 where "my sheep" refers to saved people.*

2. *Personal opinion. Jesus has a love for Christians that is amazingly strong. When a believer decides to walk in sin, the Lord will pursue him or her endlessly to return them to fellowship with Him.*

3. *Today's verses say that the shepherd announces his arrival back home to his friends and neighbors, and invites them to celebrate with him. Luke 15:7 even says that heaven rejoices also.*

## 59. WHAT DOES IT MEAN TO BE A "SON" OR "DAUGHTER?"

*"And he [the son] got up and came to his father. But while he was still a long way off, his father saw him, and felt compassion for him, and ran and embraced him, and kissed him. And the son said to him, 'Father, I have sinned against heaven and in your sight; I am no longer worthy to be called your son.'"*
*Luke 15:20, 21*

These verses are some of the tenderest, the most affectionate verses in the entire Bible—and they are some of my favorites. For one thing, they describe the depth of love God has in His huge heart for those who have put their trust in Him.

Jesus tells a story to the crowd, about a young man who insists on receiving his share of his father's inheritance, even before the father's death. He wants to leave home, be on his own, do whatever he wants, and be his own man. The son reasons, "How great it would be to not have your mother constantly asking you to clean up your bedroom—or not have your father telling you to be home by 11:00 P.M. We're talking *freedom*, man!"

But freedom didn't turn out to be what he expected. People were his friends as long as his money lasted—and then they were nowhere to be found. The only work he could find was the "lowest rung of the ladder"—feeding slop to pigs. Were people willing to genuinely love him and help him out? Verse sixteen says, "...and no one was giving anything to him."

No one cared, that is, but the father (and mother too, if she was alive). There was dad on his front porch, day after day, rain or sun, looking down the road for some sign of his son. Then one day, the father sees an approaching figure too small to identify for sure. Could it possibly be his boy? Finally he recognizes his son's walk. The father leaps off the porch and begins running down the road toward his dear one—unshaved and clothes caked with filth. The father rushes to him and gathers him in his arms, tears of love streaming down his face. Words of repentance tumble out of the son's mouth asking for forgiveness, saying, "I am no longer *worthy* to be called your son."

Notice that the father says nothing about his son's "worthiness." We are not God's children because we are worthy. Salvation is a free gift by God's grace. Romans 5:8 says, "...while we were yet sinners, Christ died for us." It's the same when we Christians wander away from our Savior and want our own independence. When we realize our sin and confess it to our heavenly Father, He forgives us (See 1 John 1:9). He runs down the road, throws His powerful arms around us, and welcomes us back into fellowship with Him. After all, we are His son or daughter, and He is our Father!

## WHAT DO YOU THINK?

1. What was the young son's mistaken understanding of "freedom"?

2. Compare the friendship of the son's companions "in the far country," with the love of his father.

3. Describe in your own words, the father's reaction when he was certain his son was repentant and was returning to the fellowship of his family.

## ANSWERS TO YOUR QUESTIONS

1. *The son thought that "freedom" was being away from his parents' authority; to be independent; to make all his own choices; to do whatever he wanted when he wanted to.*

2. *The son's companions were what is called, "fair weather friends." As long as the son was loaded with money, he was their friend. When it all ran out and he needed them, they were nowhere to be found. The father on the other hand, looked for any sign of his son's return. Even when his boy was broke, hungry, and filthy, the father welcomed him home with love and forgiveness.*

3. *Personal opinion.*

*Jealousy instead of joy*

## 60. IT'S ALL ABOUT ME

*"Now his older son was in the field, and when he came and approached the house, he heard music and dancing...But he became angry, and was not willing to go in; and his father came out and began entreating [pleading with] him."*
*Luke 15:25, 28*

When I was a teenager, I knew of a family that held such anger toward one another, that they actually divided up their home—while they were all still living there. The father died without leaving a will, so no one knew for sure who inherited the house. Instead of selling it and dividing up the money evenly among the mother, a son, and a daughter, they remodeled the house so they each had a few rooms, but also so they never ran into one another. They hated each other and they each hoped to outlive the other family members so they would inherit the whole building. Just think of all the great times they could have had together—the outdoor barbecues, and the Christmas parties. Instead, each one grew angrier and more bitter as the years rolled by. I never heard who "the last man standing" was.

It sounds like the older son in Jesus' story of the rebellious or prodigal young man would have fit into the above family very well. The father's heart was so full of joy that his younger son did not destroy himself in "a far country," but had repented of his sin and returned home. He wanted his older son to share in his joy, but the young man refused and remained outside, angry and jealous. All he could think of was that his younger brother had taken half of the father's wealth and blown it on a sinful lifestyle. His attitude was not, "My brother has returned home to the love and support of family, and I want to celebrate with my father." That would be God's attitude. Instead, it was, "It's all about *me!*"

And then the older son rattles off a list of the ways he has been faithful to the rules. Do his statements sound a lot like the Pharisees? I'm sure that was part of Jesus' intention in telling this story. The only things the elder son could think of were money and things, while the father's heart was overflowing with joy over his younger son's repentant heart and the restored fellowship that followed. One Bible teacher wisely points out, that in all three stories in Luke 15, everyone ends up happy except the older brother.[11]

Do we ever get jealous over good things that happen to other people? We really have two main choices, don't we? We can be happy for them and share in their celebration, or we can be jealous and angry, saying, "What about *me*?"

## WHAT DO YOU THINK?

1. Describe in your own words the older brother's response when he finds out that his father is putting on a huge celebration for his younger brother.

2. As we read Jesus' description of the father in this story, what do we learn about God's heart when His children repent or change their mind and attitude about their sin?

3. What was the main focus in the older son's mind? What group was he most like in attitude?

## ANSWERS TO YOUR QUESTIONS

1. *Personal opinion.*

2. *It brings great joy to God's heart when one of His children changes his mind and attitude about his sins and confesses them to God. He also wants the rest of His children to share in that joy. It grieves His heart when some believers are jealous and self-centered.*

3. *The older son was focused on himself and acted like "It's all about me," instead of being happy for his brother and sharing in his father's joy. His attitude was a lot like the Pharisees.*

*Investing in being a steward*

## 61. WHAT'S A STEWARD AND WHAT DOES SHE DO?

*Now He [Jesus] was also saying to the disciples, "There was a certain rich man who had a steward [manager],...And his master praised the unrighteous steward because he had acted shrewdly [wisely];"*
*Luke 16:1, 8*

In this parable, Jesus teaches His disciples to not just use their money for present-day pleasure, but to constantly keep eternity in mind and invest in spiritual, godly matters for the future.

Did you know you are a steward? We all are. A steward is a person who manages or takes care of someone else's wealth or property.

Let's consider how we fit this title:

- OUR TIME – We may think our time belongs to us, but God determines how little or much time we'll spend on earth (Psalm 31:15).
- OUR THOUGHTS – My mind is also not my own. If I'm a child of God, I'm responsible for what I allow into my mind (Philippians 4:8).
- OUR SPIRITUAL GIFTS – God has given each Christian certain spiritual gifts and abilities, not to make us look important, but to help the other members of the body of Christ (Romans 12:3-8).
- OUR NATURAL ABILITIES – Every person, saved or unsaved, has certain natural abilities given to her at birth by God. Some are artists, others are athletes, and still others are leaders or care-givers. These too are gifts from God (James 1:17).
- OUR MONEY – It's easy to feel that money I have earned belongs to me and no one else. It's helpful to remember that *everything* in this universe belongs to God, and I am strictly a steward of the things He gives me from His loving, generous heart (Matthew 6:25-34).

- OUR FRIENDS AND FAMILIES – Do we treat our family members and friends like a precious gift from God? That's exactly what they are (Psalm 127:3).
- OUR FUTURES – If we have trusted in Jesus as our Savior, He has guaranteed our futures. We are depending on God and His promises, not on how great we are (1 Peter 1:3-5).
- OUR DEPENDENCE ON GOD'S WORD – We are stewards of God's wonderful Word. If we don't read it, memorize it, and share it, are we really being good managers (Hebrews 4:12)?
- OUR INTIMACY WITH JESUS – The Lord Jesus waits to draw us into a deep love-relationship with Him. He pursues us, but He doesn't force us. He wants us to seek His friendship (John 15:5).
- OUR SHARING THE GOSPEL – There is no greater treasure in all the earth than the Gospel of Jesus Christ. We are stewards or managers of this message that saves souls for all eternity (2 Timothy 4:2).

Well, how does it feel to be a steward? It makes me feel valuable to God on the one hand, and also very responsible to carry out my duties well, so as to please my Master, Jesus Christ.

## WHAT DO YOU THINK?

1. What does a steward do?

2. How are we stewards or managers of our friends and family members?

3. The Lord Jesus has prepared a loving relationship between us and Him, if we have trusted Him as our Savior. What is our responsibility as stewards of this wonderful privileged friendship (See John 15:5).

## ANSWERS TO YOUR QUESTIONS

1. *A steward is a person who manages or takes care of someone else's wealth or property.*

2. *Friends and family members are a valuable gift from God. We can treat our friends, our parents, and our brothers and sisters pretty selfishly—or we can recognize that they are a treasure, given to us for our pleasure and help.*

3. *God encourages His children to "abide" in Him like a branch abides in the main trunk of a grape vine. He actively pursues us, continually inviting us to enjoy a deeper love relationship with Him. The Lord doesn't force us, but waits for us to respond to Him in faith and obedience.*

*A wrong choice can be deadly*

## 62. MAKING THE WRONG CHOICE

*"No servant can serve two masters; for either he will hate the one, and love the other, or else he will hold to one, and despise the other. You cannot serve God and mammon [riches]."*
*Luke 16:13*

Jesus continued teaching His disciples on the matter of money. He wanted them to understand that wealth is a *means* to an end—that is, paying our bills and serving the Lord. It is not an end in itself, or in other words, Christians should not just live and work to become rich and gather as much money as possible. Otherwise your bank account becomes your master or lord, instead of Jesus. Plain and simple, that is a wrong choice.

I'd like to tell you about someone else who made a wrong choice—in a very different area. It was October 25, 1964, and Jim Marshall was playing for the Minnesota Vikings football team against the San Francisco 49'ers. During the heat of the game, Jim pounced on a fumble, jumped to his feet, and raced sixty-six yards—into his own end zone.

Still unaware of his wrong choice, Jim went into his victory celebration, ending it by tossing the ball into the stands. After all, this was the only touchdown this lineman would score in his career. Because the ball went out of bounds, it counted one point for the 49'ers as a "safety." The Vikings still won the game 27-22, but this play has been called one of the most embarrassing moments in professional sports history.[12]

Was Jesus teaching the disciples that it's wrong to have money or property? Not at all. There is a difference between earning money to pay for your daily living expenses—even saving some for the future—and being a slave to your wealth. As 1 Timothy 6:10 says, "For the love of money is a root of all sorts of evil, and some by longing for it have wandered away from the faith…"

Jesus wants to be our only Lord and Master. But He can't be, if we've made gathering more wealth the whole focus of our lives.

We all remember Scrooge McDuck, a rich uncle of the Disney character, Donald Duck. Old Scrooge was disgustingly wealthy, and his favorite past-time was swimming in a pool of his gold coins. Money was his "master."[13]

When we choose to give Jesus control of our lives, He also has control of our possessions. Then it's easy for Him to prompt us to be generous with others, and to give for the spread of the Gospel to the ends of the earth.

[See also: Matthew 6:24]

## WHAT DO YOU THINK?

1. Besides running the fumbled ball into his own end zone, where did Jim Marshall first go wrong?

2. Is it wrong to work hard to earn money to pay your bills, save for the future, and even provide for some entertainment? Where does the gathering of money and possessions become sin?

3. Why do you think God wants control of every area of our lives including our wealth?

## ANSWERS TO YOUR QUESTIONS

*1. Once Jim picked up the loose ball, he had to make a choice—which direction to run.*

*2. No, it's not wrong. Working hard to earn money only becomes sin when that wealth becomes the lord and master of your life. God wants us to lay all our possessions—and our lives too—before Him so that He can use them as He desires.*

*3. First of all, as we learned earlier, everything in the universe already belongs to God. He wants us to willingly commit all we own, and our lives also, to Him for Him to use as He desires.*

*Abraham's bosom versus hell*

## 63. LAZARUS AND THE RICH MAN

*"Now it came about that the poor man [Lazarus, a believer] died and he was carried away by the angels to Abraham's bosom [heaven]; and the rich man [an unbeliever] also died and was buried. And in Hades [hell] he lifted up his eyes, being in torment, and saw Abraham far away, and Lazarus in his bosom [arms]."*
*Luke 16:22, 23*

NOTE TO PARENTS: You might want to read the whole story (Luke 16:19-31) to give the entire context.

In understanding both heaven and hell, we have to remember that God has only given us a small portion of the whole picture in His Word. He has told us enough so that we understand how to get to both places, but He still held back plenty of details. He wants us to trust Him, but also our human minds couldn't process all the information.

Luke 16:14 says, "Now the Pharisees, who were lovers of money, were listening to all these things, and they were scoffing at Him [Jesus]." So the Lord told a story which clearly illustrated their pathetic lives.

There was an unnamed rich man who probably was a picture of the Pharisees. He lived in extravagant luxury and basically ignored Lazarus who was a poor and diseased beggar at his door. Both men died, and interestingly they both carried the same amount of money and possessions into the "afterlife"—nothing!

There are differences of opinion on where each man went after death, but according to the Bible, Lazarus was carried by angels to "Abraham's bosom,"[14] and the rich man went to "Hades." It's important to realize that Lazarus did not go to a place of comfort and joy because he was *poor*, and the rich man didn't go to Hades, a place of suffering, because he was *wealthy*.

Let's first consider what we do know about these two locations. First, we'll examine "Abraham's bosom":
- Some believe it's another name for heaven.
- Others say that it's where the spirits and souls of believers go when they die, until Jesus returns for all Christians. The apostle Paul said, "...to be absent from the body and to be at home with

the Lord" (2 Corinthians 5:8). So it appears that all Christians go directly to heaven when they die. Therefore, Abraham's bosom is most likely another name for heaven given by Jesus to the Jews who were descendants of Abraham.

The rich man died and went to "Hades":
- There are those who teach that Hades is a "waiting place" for the souls and spirits of unbelievers who have died. We do know from our story that they will be in physical suffering there.
- Some others believe that Hades is another name for hell. Unbelievers remain there until the time of God's judgment on all who are unsaved.

Whatever the exact meanings are, we know from the Bible that those who trust in Jesus' shed blood will spend forever with the Lord in joy and comfort. Those who refuse to accept His free gift of salvation will spend eternity in suffering and separation from God.

## WHAT DO YOU THINK?

1. Where did the rich man go when he died? Was it because he was wealthy? Where did Lazarus go after death? Why?

2. According to the apostle Paul, where do believers' spirits go immediately after death?

3. Why do you think that God has not given us *all* the details of heaven and hell in His Word?

## ANSWERS TO YOUR QUESTIONS

1. *The rich man went to Hades when he died where he was in pain and agony, not because he was wealthy, but because he did not believe in Jesus Christ. Lazarus went to Abraham's bosom—which is another name for heaven—not because he was poor, but he trusted in Jesus as his Messiah. NOTE: We are not specifically told this about the rich man and Lazarus, but we know from many other Bible verses that there is only one way to heaven (John 14:6).*

2. *According to the apostle Paul (Philippians 1:23; 2 Corinthians 5:8), when believers die, their soul and spirit go immediately to be with Jesus Christ.*

3. *God knows how much detailed information our human minds can handle. He told us in His Word enough to know how to become a Christian believer and wants us to trust Him for the rest of the details.*

*Hell and what it's like*

## 64. WHAT HELL IS LIKE

*"And he cried out and said, 'Father Abraham, have mercy on me, and send Lazarus, that he may dip the tip of his finger in water and cool off my tongue; for I am in agony in this flame.'"*
*Luke 16:24*

    C. S. Lewis wrote a number of excellent books in addition to the Narnia series. He actually wrote a book about hell, but from a different angle. It's called *The Screwtape Letters* and the whole book is made up of letters from one senior demonic resident of hell by the name of Screwtape to his nephew Wormwood. This fictional story is advice from the more experienced Screwtape on how to defeat Christians back on earth and keep them from fulfilling God's will. Although it is a very serious subject, Lewis manages to write in an almost comical way.[15]

    The story Jesus tells the Pharisees in Luke 16 is not fictional and it is anything but comical. What true facts can we learn here about hell?

- Those who have trusted in Jesus Christ's death on Calvary's cross to pay their sin debt, are born again and will never go there. (Luke 16:22; John 5:24)
- After Christians die, they immediately go to be with the Lord Jesus where they experience joy and comfort for all eternity. (Philippians 1:23)
- When unbelievers die, they immediately experience pain and suffering, waiting for God's final judgment on them. (Luke 16:23)
- There is no "second chance" to go to heaven once an unbeliever has died. Some people teach wrongly that eventually *everyone* will arrive in heaven. These verses say just the opposite. (Luke 16:26)
- People cannot travel back from hell to earth to warn their friends how horrible hell is. (Luke 16:27, 28) [NOTE: People who say, "I don't mind going to hell since all my friends will be there," are in for a terrible surprise.]

- Even though the Bible is very clear on the reality of hell, people refuse to read and believe it. (Luke 16:31)
- If unbelievers don't accept the Bible as true—even though it's God's Word—they wouldn't even believe those who came back to life after being in hell, to warn them. (Luke 16:31)
- Jesus Christ rose from the grave after being dead for three days, and people still did not trust in Him.

Well, we have learned quite a bit about hell from today's verses. Wouldn't you rather choose heaven as a place to spend all eternity?

## WHAT DO YOU THINK?

1. Why don't those who have trusted in Christ's death on the cross to pay their sin debt, have to be concerned about landing in hell after their death?

2. Why can't unbelievers who arrive in Hades (hell) when they die, warn their friends and relatives back on earth, about the horrors of where they are?

3. Some people say that unbelievers will have a "second chance" to be saved after they die, and eventually *everyone* will be in heaven. Explain why that is incorrect.

---

## ANSWERS TO YOUR QUESTIONS

*1. God promised in His Word the Bible, that once we trust in Christ's death to pay our sin debt, we are born again, and pass from "death" to "life." (John 5:24; Hebrews 7:25)*

*2. Jesus told the Pharisees in today's verses, "...there is a great chasm [canyon] fixed, in order that those who wish to come over from here [hell] to you may not be able..." (Luke 16:26).*

*3. There is no mention in the Bible of unsaved people having a "second chance" after they die to believe in Christ. The Lord taught in today's verses that when unbelievers go to Hades (hell), they remain there. It's too late then!*

*Forgiving like Jesus forgave*

## 65. HOW MANY TIMES DO I HAVE TO FORGIVE?

*And He said to His disciples, "It is inevitable [certain] that stumbling blocks should come, but woe to him through whom they come! It would be better for him if a millstone were hung around his neck and he were thrown into the sea..."*
*Luke 17:1-4*

As Jesus approached Jerusalem, knowing He would soon be leaving the disciples to carry on God's plan on earth, He taught them in some very practical areas.

The Lord seems to have a special place in His heart for young, immature believers whom He often called "children." Jesus made it very clear how He felt towards those who cause these young ones to fall into sin or be distracted from obeying God—they would do better to be drowned in this life, and most likely will be judged later by God.

It's relatively easy to be a stumbling block or hindrance to a new Christian. Giving them too much authority too soon can lead them into pride and they fall into sin. They can be tempted through immoral choices also.

The Lord followed up the matter of being a "stumbler" to child-like believers, with teaching on "forgiveness." If we become aware of a fellow Christian choosing to walk in sin, we are responsible before God to bring it to their attention. Paul called it "speaking the truth in love..." (Ephesians 4:15).

Jesus then taught the disciples something shocking. If their Christian brother (or sister) sinned and later came to them in repentance, confessing their sin, they were bound by God's love to forgive them—an endless number of times. That shouldn't surprise us, really, because that's how Jesus forgives His children. In 1 John 1:9, we're told, "If we confess our sins, He is faithful and righteous to forgive us our sins and to cleanse us from all unrighteousness." If Jesus doesn't put a number on the times He forgives us, why should we?

I read an interesting story about *forgiveness* involving Frederick the Great, King of Prussia. He decided to visit a prison in the city of Berlin, and as he walked the halls, prisoner after prisoner yelled out his individual innocence to the king. Their messages were basically the same: "I've been a hard working, model citizen all my life, but evil men lied about me, and now I'm in prison unjustly."

There was only one man who said nothing, so the king had the guard bring this silent prisoner to him.

"Why are you here in prison?" King Frederick asked.

"I am a thief," the trembling man replied.

"Are you saying you're guilty?"

"Yes, your Majesty!"

The king called the guard over. "Set this man free and let him go home. I will not have such a guilty person corrupting all these fine, law-abiding, innocent people here in my prison."[16]

That one person was set free because he admitted that he had done wrong. In the same way, our sins are forgiven and we are set free only if we acknowledge that we have done wrong.

[See also: Matthew 18:6, 7; Mark 9:42]

# WHAT DO YOU THINK?

1. What does it mean to be a "stumbler" or "stumbling block" to immature believers in Jesus?

2. Can you think of some areas where we who are Christians can be stumbling blocks to new, young followers of Christ?

3. What was Jesus' main teaching for the disciples (and for us) about Christians who sin against us and then come in repentance and confess their sin to us?

# ANSWERS TO YOUR QUESTIONS

1. *It means that we do or say things in the presence of young believers that causes them to move away from the will of God and choose to sin.*

2. *Personal opinion. The following is one possibility—if we constantly talk to a new Christian about how important wealth and power are, we could potentially cause them to reject Christ's path and seek the attractions of this world.*

3. *Jesus' main teaching appeared to be that if a believer comes to us and in repentance confesses that he has sinned against us, we should forgive him endlessly, or without number. Jesus promises to forgive us every time we confess our sin to Him (1 John 1:9).*

*Two little words—thank you!*

## 66. A THANKER, AN IGNORER, OR A WHINER

*And as He [Jesus] entered a certain village, ten leprous men who stood at a distance met Him; and they raised their voices, saying, "Jesus, Master, have mercy on us!"...Now one of them, when he saw that he had been healed, turned back, glorifying God with a loud voice, and he fell on his face at His feet, giving thanks to Him. And he was a Samaritan.*
*Luke 17:12, 13, 15, 16*

There are many ways we could describe people's differences, and then put them into groups based on how they react to life. In today's verses, Jesus uses a dramatic encounter with ten lepers to teach His disciples how important it is to be thankful. The Lord gives no indication in His story that these lepers are believers, but for the purpose of today's devotional and to illustrate the issue of gratefulness, I would like to divide Christians into three categories, based on how they respond to God's generosity.

We'll call the first group *thankers*. I'm not talking about people who react like robots and automatically thank people without even thinking about it. I mean Christian believers who realize that as sinners, we deserve nothing from God except judgment, and that our loving Father delights in showering us with gifts for no other reason than He loves us. James says it so well: "Every good thing bestowed [given] and every perfect gift is from above, coming down from the Father of lights…" (James 1:17).

Many Christians are what I call *ignorers*. It's not that they are upset and angry—they are just so focused on their own lives that it never occurs to them that the good things they enjoy are gifts from God. The ignorers probably feel they deserve the things they have, and maybe even that they have what they have by their own hard work. Probably the nine lepers who never came back to thank Jesus for healing them were in this category.

The third group is called *whiners and complainers*. They are never quite satisfied with what they have and are determined to let everyone else know. After all, look at Joe Blow their neighbor. He's got all this stuff that's bigger and newer, and if they had the same opportunities, they would have the same or better. They are constantly comparing themselves with others.

If we are in one of the last two groups, life is basically about *me*. So why would it ever occur to us to thank someone else? The Lord Jesus is delighted when we thank Him for His kindness. Let's bring joy to His heart!

## WHAT DO YOU THINK?

1. What takes place in a Christian's heart that causes her to be truly thankful? What has she probably come to realize?

2. Why is it that *ignorers* don't seem to be aware of the tremendous blessings they have from God, and realize they should be thankful to their heavenly Father?

3. What do *whiners and complainers* often do that causes them to be so dissatisfied with what they have and are?

## ANSWERS TO YOUR QUESTIONS

1. *"Thankers" realize that as sinners, we deserve only God's judgment. Therefore, every blessing in our lives comes to us by God's grace and kindness—not by our strength and ability.*

2. *"Ignorers" tend to be focused on their own lives, and don't stop to realize that their blessings come directly from God.*

3. *"Whiners" constantly compare themselves with others who seem to have bigger and better everything. They never seem to be content with what they do have, and thankfulness to God never figures in their thinking.*

*First the suffering, then the glory*

## 67. WHEN JESUS COMES IN GLORY

*"For just as the lightning, when it flashes out of one part of the sky, shines to the other part of the sky, so will the Son of Man be in His day. But first He must suffer many things and be rejected by this generation."*
*Luke 17:24, 25*

When Jesus was talking to the Pharisees, He told them the story of the rich man and Lazarus, to try to get them to see that the Messiah—the King of the Jews—was there among them *right then.* But they didn't want what Jesus was offering them. John 1:11 says, "He came to His own [Jews], and those who were His own did not receive Him."

Now, in chapter seventeen, Jesus is talking to His disciples about His second coming in the future. (His first coming was as a baby born in Bethlehem). This is what He told them:

- They would be anxious for Jesus to return to earth after His death and resurrection. (Verse 22)
- People would be predicting exactly when the day of His return would be. The Lord said, "…do not run after them [or believe them]." (Verse 23)
- When Jesus does return, the whole world will know it, and the sky will be filled with His glorious presence—just like lightning. (Verse 24)
- Before all this glory and majesty of Jesus will be seen, He knew He had to go to the cross and suffer horribly for our sins, and die. If that wasn't bad enough, Jesus knew beforehand also, that the majority of Jews who heard His teaching would reject His free gift of salvation (Verse 25).

Just like the disciples, you may be wondering what it will be like when Jesus returns to the earth in a glorious display that this world has never witnessed before. God doesn't give us a lot of detail, but He inspired the disciple Matthew to write the following: "For just as the lightning comes from the east, and flashes even to the west, so shall the coming of the Son of Man be…and then the sign of the Son of Man will appear in the sky, and then all the tribes of the earth will mourn, and they will see the Son of Man coming on the clouds of the sky with power and great glory" (Matt 24:27, 30).

Wow! We've all seen great fireworks on the 4$^{th}$ of July, but can you imagine what kind of an event God, who created all the stars and galaxies, is planning?

We don't have to know every last detail about Christ's second coming to be at peace in our hearts. It's enough to know that we belong to Jesus because we trusted in Him, and He will make good on His promise of eternal life with Him.

[See also: Matthew 24:23-51]

## WHAT DO YOU THINK?

1. What message did Jesus have for the Pharisees?

2. Can your family together remember all four points that Jesus was teaching His disciples about his second coming, also called "His Glorious Return" to earth?

3. Why wouldn't Jesus just skip the cross with all its agony and shame, and concentrate on His glorious and powerful Second Coming?

## ANSWERS TO YOUR QUESTIONS

1. *Jesus told the Pharisees at different times and in different ways, that His "spiritual" kingdom had already come, and was there in His own person. They were looking for a Messiah who was a powerful conqueror, rather than this humble carpenter.*

2. *See the four points in the devotional.*

3. *In order for mankind to have their sins paid for, and to receive the gift of eternal life, Jesus had to go to the cross and suffer all the pain and humiliation of the crucifixion and eventually death. The glory would come after the suffering.*

*We need to be full of the Lord*

## 68. JUST TOO FULL OF ALABAMA

*"Remember Lot's wife. Whoever seeks to keep his life shall lose it, and whoever loses his life shall preserve it."*
*Luke 17:32, 33*

It was the 1954 Cotton Bowl game in Dallas, Texas, and the Rice University Owls were playing the Crimson Tide from Alabama. Rice was leading 7-6 when the Owls running back, Dickey Moegle, ran through the Tide line, and was headed down the sideline for a sure touchdown. There were no Alabama defenders between Moegle and the goal line.

Suddenly a player came off the Alabama bench as Dickey reached the 45 yard line, and dropped the ball carrier with a teeth rattling tackle. The referee awarded a touchdown to Rice.

What happened? Tommy Lewis from Alabama was sitting on the bench when he saw Moegle on his way to the end zone. When asked later why he made his famous tackle, even though he wasn't in the game, Tommy said, 'I'm just too full of Alabama!" Rice went on to win 28-6.[17]

In today's verses the Lord was specifically talking about the end of the world when He will return in all His glory. According to Revelation 1:7, every single person on earth will see Him in all His majesty, at that very same moment. But whether then or now, Jesus longs for His children to have hearts that are focused on serving Him and wanting to know Him more deeply.

In Genesis 19:12-26, we read that God was going to destroy the twin cities of Sodom and Gomorrah because they were so consumed with degrading sin. God allowed Lot (Abraham's nephew), his wife, and their two daughters to escape the fiery judgment on Sodom, but he told them to flee and *not look back*. As they made their way to the town of Zoar, Lot's wife looked back. Did she miss all the nice things she owned back home? Was she wishing she could go back to life in the corrupt city of Sodom? It appears she was double-minded. Part of her wanted to escape the coming destruction and part of her wanted to go back to the life she experienced in Sodom.

God judged Lot's wife by turning her into a pillar of salt. She had directly disobeyed God.

Tommy Lewis was "too full of Alabama." Lot's wife was "too full of Sodom." The Lord Jesus desires us to focus fully on Him, determine to know His will, and do it.

Remember Lot's wife!

[See also: Matthew 10:38, 39; 16:25; Mark 8:35; Luke 9:23; John 12:25, 26]

## WHAT DO YOU THINK?

1. What does it mean that Lot's wife was double-minded?

2. How could we as born again Christians be like Lot's wife?

3. Luke 9:62 says, "But Jesus said to him, 'No one, after putting his hand to the plow and looking back, is fit for the kingdom of God.'" How would this verse apply to today's verses?

## ANSWERS TO YOUR QUESTIONS

1. *Lot's wife's mind was working in two directions. On the one hand, she was determined to flee from Sodom when she heard that God was going to destroy that city. On the other, she seemed to long to return to the old familiar pleasures of her corrupt home town.*

2. *Personal opinion. You could be a born again Christian and attend all kinds of church services and youth group activities. You could know all the "right things to say" when you're around other Christians. But when you are away from church and home, you could be longing to be just like unbelievers in what you do and think.*

3. *Personal opinion. Jesus wants His born again children to be "single-minded"—that is focused on serving Him and getting to know Him more deeply. He wants to be the source of our joy and pleasure and not have us constantly turning back to the world.*

*Pray continually!*

## 69. FAITH TO PRAY

*Now He was telling them a parable to show that at all times they ought to pray and not to lose heart,..."However, when the Son of Man comes, will He find faith on the earth?"*
*Luke 18:1, 8*

Luke chapter 18 is a wonderful record of Jesus teaching His disciples about "faith," and what it means in the Christian's life. In these next four devotionals, we will read about four different aspects of "faith" and how they affect our everyday lives.

The word *faith* gets used so often on TV, in movies, and the written media, that it has lost much of its meaning. I often hear a TV news anchor talking about an athlete or celebrity, and the announcer will say, "She is a good person and her 'faith' is important to her."

What does that mean? Faith, here, could mean anything from "faith in herself" to "witchcraft" to "Zen Buddhism." It rarely means trust in Jesus Christ alone—at least in the media.

The closer Jesus got to Calvary and His death on the cruel Roman cross, the more we read of the Lord preparing His disciples. Very soon He would be back in heaven and they would be involved in taking the Good News to the rest of the world—without His physical presence.

What did Jesus tell them about prayer? First, He told them that they should pray *at all times*. I don't think He meant that twenty-four hours a day, the disciples—and we today—should be constantly praying. Our Savior desires His children to be in a right attitude of heart where we have constant fellowship with Him during every waking hour.

I find that prayer in my own life is becoming that. I still have times of prayer (usually in the morning) where I will go through a list of prayer requests and items of praise. But I'm more conscious of Jesus being right with me throughout the day. I was looking at a beautiful tiger lily flower the other day, and I found myself thanking the Lord for it in my mind and praising Him for His amazing creative power.

Other times, when I am puzzled over what decision to make, I'll just start talking to Jesus about it, asking Him for His help. Prayer is becoming an on-going, all-day discussion with my heavenly Father.

In today's verses, the Lord was not only teaching His disciples to keep praying about issues that were on their hearts—to be persistent. He also urged them to pray "with faith" that God hears their prayers and will answer them according to His own will rather than our schedule.

Do you get the idea that our dear Lord Jesus loves to have fellowship with us—as often as we can?

## WHAT DO YOU THINK?

1. On TV in particular, we often hear about a celebrity's "faith." What does that mean?

2. What was Jesus meaning when He said that men (or all born again people) should pray "at all times."

3. Describe in your own words what Jesus most likely meant when He told His disciples "that they ought to pray and not to lose heart."

## ANSWERS TO YOUR QUESTIONS

*1. The media talk about people's faith, and it could mean anything from faith or confidence in themselves to trust in pagan gods.*

*2. God obviously doesn't mean that we should pray during every minute we are awake throughout the day. He desires a loving relationship with us that continues throughout the day, where we not only ask Him for His help, but we discuss with Him the thoughts in our minds.*

*3. God wants us to trust Him after we ask Him to do something. If His answer doesn't come right away, the Lord wants us to keep asking Him with confidence that He will answer according to His schedule.*

## 70. FAITH FOR SALVATION

*And He also told this parable to certain ones who trusted in themselves that they were righteous, and viewed others with contempt:... "But the tax-gatherer, standing some distance away, was even unwilling to lift up his eyes to heaven, but was beating his breast [chest], saying, 'God, be merciful to me, the sinner!'"*
*Luke 18:9, 13*

It's amazing to me that in so many areas of life and truth, God's ways are the exact opposite to what we hear and see around us every day. You could say that His thinking is 180 degrees in the opposite direction from most of our thinking.

I talked recently with a young lady (we'll call her Linda) and I asked her the same question I often ask people when I get the opportunity, "If you were to die suddenly, you found yourself standing before God, and He asked you, 'Why should I allow you into heaven?' what would you say to Him?"

Linda's answer was sadly similar to how so many people answer that same question: "I think I have tried hard to be a *good person,* so I think God realizes that and will allow me into heaven when I die."

What is the main problem with Linda's thinking? (PARENTS: You may want to stop here and allow your children to share their opinions.)

Think of a high jumper in a track meet. At the very beginning the bar is low, and all the competitors can clear the bar easily. That's kind of the way most people think of their own righteousness or goodness. Linda set the bar low in her life and felt that she had easily met all of her own requirements to enter heaven. As she looked at her life, despite all the self-centeredness and disobedience to God, she was sure that she was good enough for heaven. Linda felt she had cleared the bar.

But God sets the bar at the level of *perfection.* It's impossible for any of us to "jump that high"—and that's the very reason Jesus came to earth, died on the cross, and rose again. We need His shed blood to pay for our sins—our "goodness" isn't good enough.

In this parable that Jesus told, the tax-collector understood this fact. He didn't pretend that he had "tried hard enough" and had cleared the bar easily to go to heaven. He clearly realized that he was unworthy and needed God's grace.

The Pharisee was another story. He even had the nerve to list off to God in his prayer what a great guy he was. After all, look how many good things he was doing. He failed to see that salvation is all about Jesus Christ and what He has done, and not about how worthy we are.

Where are you setting the bar?

## WHAT DO YOU THINK?

1. What question does the author often ask people concerning salvation and how do they usually answer?

2. Linda's problem was that she "set the bar" too low for her own righteousness. What does that mean?

3. Why was the tax-collector accepted before God, while the religious Pharisee was not?

## ANSWERS TO YOUR QUESTIONS

1. *The question is, "If you were to die suddenly, you found yourself standing before God, and He asked you, 'Why should I allow you into heaven?' what would you say to Him?" Most people answer that they believe they deserve to go to heaven because of all the good things they have done. They ignore all their selfishness and disobedience.*

2. *God's standard is "perfection" because He is holy and without sin, and can't permit sin of any kind in His presence. Linda was satisfied with the few "good deeds" she had done, and felt that God should be satisfied also. That is lowering the bar of what's necessary for heaven.*

3. *The tax-collector humbled himself by admitting that because of his sin, he was unworthy of heaven and deserved only God's punishment. The Pharisee was full of himself. He couldn't see any reason to depend only in God's free gift.*

*The best thing of all*

## 71. FAITH FOR GOD'S FELLOWSHIP

*And a certain ruler questioned Him [Jesus], saying, "Good Teacher, what shall I do to inherit eternal life?"...And he [the ruler] said, "All these things I have kept from my youth." And when Jesus heard this, He said to him, "One thing you still lack;..."*
Luke 18:18, 21, 22

What would you say is the "one thing" Jesus wanted for the crowds of people generally, and for the rich young ruler specifically? It seems obvious that He wanted them to experience forgiveness of their sins through faith in Him, and eternal life as one of His children.

When this wealthy young man of influence asks Jesus what he has to do to inherit eternal life, he was probably thinking of more laws to keep. The Lord knew his heart and understood that this young man not only treasured his wealth above everything, but was badly misguided about his own righteousness. He was sure he had kept every last one of God's laws since his childhood. What other laws could there possibly be?

Hearing the pride oozing from this ruler of Israel, Jesus cut to the chase and quickly diagnosed the man's need—"One thing you still lack." What could that possibly be? He had never seen himself as a condemned sinner in need of the Savior, Jesus. He was obviously depending on his own good works—and he enjoyed being wealthy as well.

Jesus, knowing that the young man's heart was wrapped around his immense bank account, He challenged him to sell all his wealth, give it to the poor, and follow Him. Would selling off his gold and silver save him? Of course not. But instead of depending on his wealth and good behavior for salvation, and following Christ, he would be demonstrating repentance (a change of mind). It would not be long, then, in the company of Jesus that he would hear and understand that Jesus was the Messiah, and that by trusting in His soon-to-be sacrifice on the cross, he would definitely "inherit eternal life."

To summarize, then, what did Jesus mean when He told the proud young ruler, "One thing you still lack"? The Lord meant that he lacked eternal salvation because his heart belonged to his wealth and he was depending on his own good works to earn his way to heaven.

Can you think of other things that people depend on to inherit eternal life, other than trusting in Jesus Christ?

[See also: Matthew 19:16-30; Mark 10:17-31]

## WHAT DO YOU THINK?

1. What was the "one thing" that Jesus desired for the crowds of people generally, and for the rich young ruler specifically?

2. How did the young man measure himself as far as obeying the whole Law of Moses?

3. How did his initial question to Jesus reveal where he was spiritually?

## ANSWERS TO YOUR QUESTIONS

1. *Jesus desired that they would realize they were lost sinners and believe in His sacrifice to pay for their sins.*

2. *The rich young man believed that he had totally obeyed the Law of Moses since his childhood.*

3. *The very fact that he asked Jesus what he had to "do" rather than what he had to "believe" revealed that he was looking in the wrong direction.*

*Jesus always did the Father's will*

## 72. FAITH TO TRUST WHAT GOD SAYS

*And He took the twelve aside and said to them, "Behold, we are going up to Jerusalem, and all things which are written through the prophets about the Son of Man will be accomplished. For He will be delivered to the Gentiles, and will be mocked and mistreated and spit upon, and after they have scourged Him, they will kill Him; and the third day He will rise again." And they understood none of these things,...*
Luke 18:31-34

I've heard a number of people say something like, "I believe in God, but I'm not sure that Jesus is God also. He may have been a good teacher who lived 2,000 years ago, but God...I don't think so."

Ravi Zacharias, a wonderful Bible teacher who grew up in India, tells a true story that illustrates the relationship between God the Father and Jesus Christ, God the Son. He told of a father and son who were world-famous for making wedding saris—beautiful, richly colorful gowns of sheer texture that Asian women would wear on their wedding day.

Rather than having the latest in computer-enhanced machinery, or a production line of master weavers, there were only the two family members—and the father sat on a platform above the son, surrounded by spools of thread. It was the father who decided what colors he wanted, and the son depended solely on the father's wisdom and expertise. The older man would simply nod at a particular moment, and the son would move the shuttle back and forth.

Little by little, over dozens of hours, a beautiful sari with intricate patterns in gold and silver thread would begin to take form. And all the time it was a creation of the father's heart.[18]

When Jesus was on earth, He was both God and man, with a physical body like ours. Though equal with the Father (see Hebrews 1:3), while on earth He totally submitted His will to that of His Father. He alone was the "master weaver" of Christ's activities while the Savior walked our world. Jesus said, "My food [My entire spiritual diet] is to do the will of Him who sent Me, and to accomplish His work" (John 4:34).

Since Jesus rose from the grave and returned to God the Father's side in heaven, the triune (three person) God—Father, Son, and Holy Spirit—work in total unity and harmony. They are equal in power, authority, and glory, in ways that our human minds cannot understand.

And why do we believe this marvelous truth, even though we don't fully understand it? Because it is written over and over in God's Word.

In today's verses, Jesus' disciples still struggled to understand who their Master was. Verse 34 says that a full understanding of the person of Christ was *hidden from them*. On the other hand, the Lord told them repeatedly that He had to go to Jerusalem and die, and I wonder if they believed Him completely.

I find at times that I struggle to simply believe and trust in what God's Word says. Do you experience that too?

[See also: Matthew 16:21; 20:17-19; Mark 10:32-34]

## WHAT DO YOU THINK?

1. Explain how the relationship between God the Father and Jesus Christ, during the Son's time on earth, is illustrated by the father-son team of world famous weavers in today's devotional.

2. Who is the Trinity and how do they relate to each other in power, authority, and glory?

3. How can we see ourselves in the way that the disciples constantly tried to figure out who exactly Jesus was, and what He was up to?

## ANSWERS TO YOUR QUESTIONS

1. *Jesus said repeatedly that while on earth, He only did what God the Father directed Him to do. His "spiritual food" was to do the Father's will. As far as the weavers, the father knew what form he wanted the wedding sari to take. He sat above his son and directed every aspect of the pattern and combination of colors. The son constantly looked to his father for direction.*

2. *The Trinity is made up of God the Father, God the Son, and God the Holy Spirit. They are equal in power, authority, and glory.*

3. *The disciples struggled to understand who Jesus was and if in fact He was the long-awaited Messiah. Luke writes that full understanding was "hidden from them" by the Lord, but they still did not just believe His word that He was going to Jerusalem to die on the cross. We all struggle at times believing God's promises. One example would be that we are told in the Bible: "Be anxious for nothing..." (Philippians 4:6), but we still worry and fret.*

## 73. GOD CONSTANTLY SEEKS THE LOST

*"For the Son of Man has come to seek and to save that which was lost."*

*Luke 19:10*

Have you ever hunted for something valuable that you lost, and you just never gave up looking for it? In our family, just the phrase "the blue topaz ring" brings back the memory of a lovely topaz ring I gave my wife.

During our time as missionaries in Panama, President Noriega was becoming more defiant of the USA and threatened all Americans in his country. We expected the US military to invade and overthrow this dangerous man. My wife Del had to make a brief trip back to the US to care for her sick mother, and on her return was landing at the Panama City airport. She thought the customs officials there might take her topaz ring, so she put it in a pill case in her purse.

Later, she forgot she had done this in a hurried moment, and thought she had lost it. Del looked everywhere she could think of in the weeks following her trip—but no ring. I felt so bad for her, and so I secretly arranged with one of my daughters—who was coming home to Panama for Christmas from college—to buy an identical ring. I tied the new ring in a cluster of mistletoe and hung it from the ceiling.

On Christmas Eve, I led my wife under the mistletoe to kiss her, and when we were directly under it, I said, "Now look up!" When her eyes focused on the blue topaz stone, she screamed, "Where did you find it?" Of course I didn't find it. This was a new ring exactly like the original.

Four years later, when we were packing to move back to the USA, Del found the first ring in the unused pill box. She had never stopped looking for that ring.

Today's verse tells us so much about Jesus' attitude toward unsaved people. He isn't an indifferent, disinterested deity who busies Himself in heaven, while we struggle here on earth to try and discover who God is and what He wants from us. God's Word tells us that He loves mankind so deeply that He was willing to go to

Calvary and be beaten, spit upon, humiliated, and finally crucified, so that all humanity could be saved and spend eternity with Him in heaven.

The apostle Peter wrote, "The Lord is not slow about His promise, as some count slowness, but is patient toward you, not wishing for any to perish but for all to come to repentance" (2 Peter 3:9).

What a wonderful God He is, who longs so much to have every person join Him in heaven that He aggressively seeks after them, urging them to trust in His beloved Son.

[See also: Matthew 18:11]

## WHAT DO YOU THINK?

1. Have you ever lost something that was so valuable and precious to you that you never stopped looking for it? PARENTS: Each of these questions can make for an extended discussion with your children.

2. Explain in your own words what it means that "the Son of Man has come to seek and to save that which was lost."

3. What does it tell you about your value to God, that He never stops pursuing you until you become His child by faith in Christ.

## ANSWERS TO YOUR QUESTIONS

1. *Personal opinion.*

2. *Personal opinion.*

3. *Personal opinion.*

*Jesus officially enters Jerusalem*

## 74. JESUS' GRAND ENTRANCE INTO JERUSALEM

*And as He was going, they were spreading their garments in the road. And as He was now approaching, near the descent of the Mount of Olives, the whole multitude of the disciples began to praise God joyfully with a loud voice for all the miracles which they had seen, saying, "Blessed is the King who comes in the name of the Lord; peace in heaven and glory in the highest!"*
*Luke 19:36-38*

The most powerful and painful final act of the greatest drama ever to take place on earth involving God's Son, Jesus Christ, is about to burst onto the stage of the dusty streets of Jerusalem. The audience is hushed. The orchestra waits to explode into instrumental praise. The lights go down, the curtain parts, and the greatest love story ever told is about to begin.

No, this is not an outdoor theatre with actors portraying *The Passion of the Christ*. This is real life! All of Jesus' thirty years on earth have pointed Him toward this day, and now He is about to enter Jerusalem in order to lay down His life to pay for the sins of all mankind.

Imagine we are there on that day. It's brutally hot and we're standing by the gate to Jerusalem, waiting for Jesus to make his entrance. There He is, slowly approaching from the direction of the Mount of Olives. He is riding on a small colt and in front of Him, people are laying down their cloaks so the colt doesn't have to step on the ground. All around us we hear His disciples shouting, "Blessed is the King who comes in the name of the Lord," a quote from Psalm 118:26.

What is the significance of this strange but majestic moment? Jesus is presenting Himself to the Jewish people (including the religious leaders) as their King, just as Zechariah 9:9 prophesied: "Rejoice greatly, O daughter of Zion! Shout in triumph, O daughter of Jerusalem! Behold, your king is coming to you; He is just and endowed with salvation, humble, and mounted on a donkey, even on a colt, the foal of a donkey."

Some of the people are anticipating that this "King of the Jews"—if in fact He is—will overthrow their Roman conquerors.

Others expect Him to at least set up a throne in this great commercial city, from where He will reign.

Why would the people be shouting, "Peace in heaven"? Wasn't God's peace needed here on earth? Wasn't that why the Messiah came—so that as the King of the Jews, He would reign over mankind with peace and righteousness and justice? Surely, all Jews will have a special place of favor in His kingdom. How is this drama going to play out? Will the religious leaders accept Jesus as their king? Read on to find out!

[See also: Matthew 21:1-11; Mark 11:1-11; John 12:12-19]

## WHAT DO YOU THINK?

1. Why did Jesus instruct His disciples to get a donkey colt for Him to ride into Jerusalem? Wouldn't a huge white stallion look more majestic and kingly?

2. Explain in your own words the significance of this moment in time when Jesus was riding into Jerusalem.

3. What do you think the Jewish people expected Jesus to do once He entered the city of Jerusalem?

## ANSWERS TO YOUR QUESTIONS

*1. Jesus was fulfilling prophecy as spoken hundreds of years before in Zechariah 9:9 which clearly states that He would enter Jerusalem "...mounted on a donkey, even on a colt, the foal of a donkey." The Lord was more interested in obeying the Word of God than He was in trying to impress the people by the size of His transportation.*

*2. Personal opinion.*

*3. Personal opinion. Luke doesn't actually say, but if He was coming to offer Himself to the nation of Israel, then the Jewish people would obviously expect Him to do what kings normally do—overthrow the conquering Roman government; take over the biggest building in the city and make that His palace; build up a huge army; and appoint a whole host of leaders and associates.*

*Jesus is worthy of praise and glory*

## 75. WHEN EVEN THE ROCKS SING

*And some of the Pharisees in the multitude said to Him [Jesus], "Teacher, rebuke Your disciples." And He answered and said, "I tell you, if these [people] become silent, the stones will cry out!"*
Luke 19:39, 40

What a thrilling historical moment this was! Jesus, God's beloved Son, was entering the great city of Jerusalem, riding on a colt of a donkey. Finally, He was openly declaring Himself as Israel's king, to the cheers and praises of His disciples. Will the Pharisees understand the prophetic significance of this moment and join the throng of worshipers in praise?

Obviously not! You can just picture groups of scribes, Pharisees, Sadducees—maybe even the high priest—looking down from the windows of their expensive mansions, with hatred in their hearts. They had heard of this carpenter from the backwoods of Galilee, who claimed to be God's Son. They had even watched Him heal the lame and the blind—must be some type of magic.

But what was happening now in Jerusalem was certainly not what they would have planned. They were losing control of the hearts of more and more Jewish people.

All along, they planned to kill this troublemaker, but they didn't want to do it on the Passover Feast. Wasn't it their responsibility to protect the Jewish people and keep them from being deceived by all the religious charlatans (deceivers) that come along?

Yes, the religious leaders understood very well the significance of Jesus' triumphant entry into Jerusalem as the King of the Jews. They would do away with this "pretender," but would wait until the annual celebration was over. Then they would deal with this "so-called king." (See Matthew 26:1-5)

But the Father's plan was that Jesus would die on the cross on the very day of the Passover. Since the days of Moses, Jews celebrated this day—off and on—by sacrificing an unblemished (undamaged) lamb for each family. Now the Son of God is about to fulfill John the Baptist's prophecy. John 1:36 records His words of hope, "Behold, the Lamb of God!" Four thousand years of history have passed since God first promised Abraham that a Messiah would come from his descendants, and now it was about to be fulfilled.

Did the Pharisees and their cronies receive Jesus as their king along with Christ's rejoicing disciples? Not at all! They only rebuked the Lord for allowing people to give Him glorious praise and call Him their king.

How did the Lord Jesus respond? He humbly but firmly told them that someone or something had to give Him praise at this glorious moment. If people were not allowed to rejoice, God would make the very stones in the road sing His praises. The hearts of the Pharisees were obviously harder than the rocks they were standing on.

[See also: Matthew 21:15-17]

## WHAT DO YOU THINK?

1. The Pharisees hated Jesus and must have been infuriated by the Jewish people praising Him and calling Him their king. Why do you think they hated the Lord so much? After all, they were experts on the Old Testament Scriptures.

2. Why did the Pharisees and other religious officials not want to kill Jesus on the Passover Feast? (See Matthew 26:1-5)

3. What did Jesus mean when He told the Pharisees, "If these [people] become silent, the stones will cry out" (Luke 19:40)?

## ANSWERS TO YOUR QUESTIONS

1. *Personal opinion. During the three years of Jesus' preaching, He constantly exposed the Pharisees and scribes for their hypocrisy. They paraded around like they were powerful religious leaders, and yet they committed all kinds of sin because of their proud hearts. On top of that, they were jealous of God's Son and wanted to destroy Him.*

2. *According to Matthew's account, they were afraid to kill Jesus on the day of the Passover Feast for fear of causing a riot in Jerusalem.*

3. *Jesus was saying that this was a day of rejoicing because the Messiah was officially presenting Himself to the Jewish people. If the Pharisees were able to keep the people from shouting Christ's praises, God would make the stones alongside the road praise Him.*

*Jesus cries over the people of Jerusalem*

## 76. THE DAY JESUS CRIED

*And when He approached [Jerusalem], He saw the city and wept over it, saying, "If you had known in this day, even you, the things which make for peace! But now they have been hidden from your eyes."*

*Luke 19:41, 42*

What was Jesus doing as He rode closer to the city of Jerusalem, even while the people were shouting His praises? He was weeping! That seems a little strange, doesn't it? The more we get to know our Savior through carefully reading His Word, the more sense it makes.

Despite the fact that His closest followers were praising Him, He knew the hearts of the majority of the Jewish people—especially the religious leaders. They wanted nothing to do with Him, and definitely not as their king—they just wanted to explore ways to kill Him without getting into trouble with their Roman rulers. They had three years to receive Him as their long-awaited Messiah, and all they wanted from Him was food for their stomachs and miraculous healings for their friends.

We all cry for different reasons, don't we? Peter wept out of *regret* when he realized that he had denied his Savior—not once, but three times. (See Matthew 26:75)

Jesus shed tears of *compassion and concern* when He was with His friends Mary and Martha at the death of their brother Lazarus. (See John 11:35)

There by the tomb where Jesus was buried following His crucifixion, Mary Magdalene sobbed tears of *love* for her Savior, thinking that He was gone forever. (See John 20:13)

Some people even cry out of *anger* when they can't have their own way.

I cry easily, so the times of my weeping are too numerous to count. I think I will always remember one particular time when I was about twelve. It was a Friday night and I told my parents that I wanted to attend the local high school football game. But I lied to them. I really wanted to go to the movies.

About half-way through the movie, my heart was so heavy with the *guilt* of having deceived my parents that I left the theatre, jumped on a bus, and headed for the football game. I can still remember running from the bus stop to the game with tears streaming down my face, feeling so rotten for having lied to my dad and mom. And they had trusted my word!

As Jesus rode into Jerusalem that historic day, He wept over the *hardness of the Jewish people's hearts*. He knew that in a few short years, the Roman army would destroy the city and the temple, and the Jewish people would pay a steep price for rejecting their king.

## WHAT DO YOU THINK?

1. What are your thoughts about "crying"? Does it show a weak and childish personality?

2. Why was Jesus crying as He rode into Jerusalem on the back of a colt, even while so many were shouting His praises?

3. Can you remember a time in your life when you cried: out of a loving concern for another person; out of regret for something wrong you did; or out of pure love for someone dear to you? PARENTS: It may take a little longer to draw your children out on this topic, but it should be worth the time and effort.

## ANSWERS TO YOUR QUESTIONS

1. *Personal opinion.*

2. *Jesus had a deep love for the nation of Israel, and although a few people were honoring Him with their praises, the majority of the Jewish people, including the religious leaders, refused to accept Him as their Savior and king.*

3. *Personal opinion.*

## 77. COUNTDOWN TO CALVARY

*And it came about on one of the days while He was teaching the people in the temple and preaching the gospel, that the chief priests and the scribes with the elders confronted Him.*
*Luke 20:1*

The clock was ticking! Jesus' final week before His savage death on the cross was underway. The count-down had begun!

SUNDAY (Day 5) – The Lord Jesus entered the city of Jerusalem seated on the colt of a donkey, amidst the praise and celebration of His disciples. But as He rode through the gate, tears of love flowed down His bearded face, recognizing that those same shouts of praise would soon turn into demands of "Crucify Him!"

MONDAY (Day 4) – Mark gives an excellent account of this very active day. "And they [Jesus and His disciples] came to Jerusalem. And He entered the temple and began to cast out those who were buying and selling in the temple, and overturned the tables of the moneychangers and the seats of those who were selling doves; and He would not permit anyone to carry goods through the temple. And He began to teach and say to them, 'Is it not written, "My house shall be called a house of prayer for all the nations"? But you have made it a robbers' den.'... And whenever evening came, they would go out of the city" (Mark 11:15-17, 19).

Can't you just picture this scene? God's temple that was built according to His own specifications had become an enormous flea market—a religious mall where you could buy almost anything. Greedy money-changers and those who sold doves for sacrifices were cheating the worshipers—and the Pharisees, no doubt, were getting their share of the pot.

I love to picture this scene in my mind. Jesus begins at one entrance and starts turning over tables and pushing shady venders toward the exits. The air is filled with dust and feathers. This is a side of the Savior that is totally new to the disciples, and I'm sure their mouths were hanging open. The Son of God was clearing this den of thieves out of His Father's house of worship! It almost makes you want to cheer.

TUESDAY (Day 3) – How the Jewish religious leaders hated Jesus! He was starting to really mess up their plans. Here they were in charge of the whole religious system that had existed since the days of Moses. They were held in high respect as they swished around Jerusalem in their easily recognized Pharisaic robes.

"We are the authorities on the Law," they likely snarled. "Who does this uneducated carpenter think He is disrupting things? Besides, after yesterday's 'display' in the temple, it's starting to affect our wallets! We've got to get rid of Him."

[See also: Matthew 21:23-23:37; Mark 11:27-12:44]

# WHAT DO YOU THINK?

1. Describe in your own words the scene in the temple courtyard on "day four" of Christ's final week before His death.

2. Since the chief priests, the scribes (Pharisees and Sadducees), and the elders, were the experts on the Old Testament, why do you think they didn't understand that the Messiah was coming and Jesus was fulfilling all the prophecies of this "Expected One"?

3. Hundreds of years before Jesus was on earth, the prophet Jeremiah wrote on behalf of God, "Why then has this people, Jerusalem, turned away in continual apostasy [untruth]? They hold fast to deceit [lies], they refuse to return [to Me]...no man repented of his wickedness..." (Jeremiah 8:5, 6). How does that apply to those days of Jesus' entry into Jerusalem also?

# ANSWERS TO YOUR QUESTIONS

1. *Personal opinion.*

2. *Although they knew the Old Testament Law in their heads, they had never humbled their own hearts and trusted in God to forgive their sins and save them. They were proud of their religious position; they were jealous of Jesus and His impact on the Jewish people; their hearts were hardened in their sins; and they could only think of themselves.*

3. *Personal opinion. The nation of Israel and specifically the people of their major city of Jerusalem had not changed since Jeremiah's time, despite having the Old Testament Scriptures, the prophets, and now God's own Son.*

## 78. WHO'S YOUR BOSS?

*...and they [chief priests etc.] spoke, saying to Him [Jesus], "Tell us by what authority You are doing these things, or who is the one who gave You this authority?" And He answered and said to them, "I shall also ask you a question, and you tell Me: was the baptism of John from heaven or from men?"*
*Luke 20:2-4*

Not only are the days counting down to Jesus' crucifixion, but Luke explains clearly how the religious leaders have become more harsh and accusatory to the Lord. They are determined to find some Roman law He has broken, so they can say, "See! Right there! He broke that law. Let's report Him!"

One thing about "pride" is that it blinds your common sense. The chief priests, the scribes (made up of Pharisees and Sadducees), and elders thought they could match wits with Jesus, the Creator of everything (including them), and somehow back Him into a corner where He would break the Law. How foolish of them!

These Jewish religious leaders were obviously enraged when Jesus cleared out the temple of all the shady characters and turned over their tables. Who did he think He was acting like this in *their* temple? So, they decide to ask Him two questions. They probably met together all night to come up with these clever thoughts.

The first question was by what authority Jesus took these unheard of actions in the temple. Was He a prophet? Was He a priest of some secret order? Did He seriously think that He was the King of the Jews? They were sneakily trying to trick the Lord into making some outrageous claim to authority, and then they could pounce on Him. Can't you just picture them all hovering around Jesus like a flock of buzzards, twisting their beards on their fingers, hoping for that moment when they could say, "Hah! We've got you!"

Their next question was loaded with trickery as well: "Who is the one who gave you this authority?" In other words, they wanted to pin Jesus down to say who was behind Him—whom did He represent? Who was His boss?

The Lord Jesus, the beloved Son of God, the Creator of the Universe, Jehovah in the Highest, simply asked these bogus leaders this simple question: "Was the baptism of John from heaven or from men?" The chief priests and their cronies immediately put their heads together hoping through their collective wisdom to come back with a brilliant answer that would make the Lord look foolish. The best they could do was admit that they themselves were trapped in a box.

They realized that there was no way they could answer Jesus' question. If they admitted that John's baptism was of God, why then did they not accept it as truth? If they said it was of men, the Jewish people would turn against them and likely stone them because they believed John was a prophet. Once again the Son of God defeated the opposition 1-0!

[See also: Matthew 21:23-27; Mark 11:27-33]

## WHAT DO YOU THINK?

1. Why did the religious leaders in Jerusalem keep asking Jesus questions?

2. What action on Jesus' part seemed to be the final straw that pushed these leaders over the edge and convinced them they had to destroy Jesus?

3. Jesus, the Son of God, asked the chief priests, Pharisees, and Sadducees a simple question. What was it and why did they not feel they could answer?

## ANSWERS TO YOUR QUESTIONS

1. *The religious leaders thought they were very clever and that by asking Jesus "tough questions" they could get Him to say something against the law, and then report Him to the Roman authorities. Their goal was to destroy Jesus.*

2. *It seems that when Jesus cleared all the crooks, money-changers, and scoundrels out of the temple, the religious leaders became more aggressive in their attacks on the Lord.*

3. *Jesus asked, "Was the baptism of John from heaven or from men?" If the leaders said it was of heaven, then the obvious next question would be, "Then why did you not believe him?" If they said John's baptism was strictly of men, then the Jewish crowd would likely turn on them and stone them because they believed John was a prophet from God.*

## 79. THE HUMAN BRAIN VERSUS THE COMPUTER

*And the scribes and the chief priests tried to lay hands on Him that very hour, and they feared the people; for they understood that He spoke this parable against them. And they watched Him, and sent spies who pretended to be righteous, in order that they might catch Him in some statement, so as to deliver Him up to the rule and the authority of the governor.*
Luke 20:19, 20

Which is smarter, a man's brain or a computer? Earlier this year there was a contest on TV to try and answer that question.

The very popular quiz show *Jeopardy* arranged for the two top winners on their program—Ken Jennings, who won the most games in a row (74 games and $2.5 million) and Brad Rutter, who won the most money ($3,255,102.00)—to compete in a three day series against the specially programmed IBM computer called "Watson", after the founder of IBM, Thomas Watson.

The contest was set for February 14-16, 2011. There were a couple of times when the men drew close to Watson, but at the end of the third day, Watson had won $77,147.00, Jennings took second with $24,000.00, and Rutter was third with $21,600.00. The computer had triumphed over the two men by a wide margin.

There was only one choice that Watson made that left everyone scratching their heads. Under the category of *American Cities*, the three were given the clue, "Its largest airport is named for a World War 2 *hero*; its second largest for a World War 2 *battle*." Both men answered correctly "Chicago," but Watson gave the name of a major *Canadian* city, "Toronto." Even computers have their times when they are distracted.[19]

During Jesus' time of ministry on earth, the high priests, scribes, and elders thought they were smarter than the Lord. Pride blinded their minds. They were sure they could trick him into saying something illegal—then they could report Him to the Roman government, who would then do their dirty work for them.

How foolish they were! Jesus Christ, the Son of God, created every star and every planet in the heavens. He spoke and every flower, animal, and drop of water came into being. Jesus even created every nerve cell in the brains of these religious leaders. And yet they thought they could trap Jesus into making a mistake. What fools they were!

I'm so thankful that I can depend on the Lord Jesus Christ—who is omniscient (knows everything)—when I need His help.

[See also: Matthew 22:15-22; Mark 12:13-17]

# WHAT DO YOU THINK?

1. Because Watson, the IBM computer, beat the two men on *Jeopardy*, do you think that means the computer is more intelligent, wiser, and more complex than the human brain? PARENTS: This could be a good discussion question for the whole family to participate in.

2. What convinced the religious leaders that they were smarter than Jesus and could trap Him into condemning Himself?

3. How do we as God's children benefit from the fact that God is omniscient or knows everything?

⁓∞⁓

# ANSWERS TO YOUR QUESTIONS

1. *Watson was programmed to give correct answers to possibly millions of questions. A computer is not more complex than the human brain. Besides remembering an innumerable number of facts, the brain can make wise decisions; can love with deep emotions and feelings; can be kind and caring to a hurting person; and can worship our heavenly Father. We are made in the image of God, whereas computers were put together with human wisdom given by God.*

2. *Human pride blinded the hearts and minds of the religious leaders. They thought more highly of themselves than they should have, even to the place of believing they were more clever than the Creator of the universe.*

3. *We can go to God any time we need His help, and ask Him for wisdom and guidance. (See James 1:5)*

*Jesus' courage and the Pharisees' cowardice*

## 80. WHERE DOES COURAGE COME FROM?

*And some of the scribes answered and said, "Teacher, You have spoken well." For they did not have courage to question Him [Jesus] any longer about anything.*
*Luke 20:39, 40*

What is *courage* all about? It obviously was not the Pharisees' and Sadducees' main strength. Even in their trickery and mob madness, they were afraid of the people, and so they didn't follow through with their evil plan to seize Jesus.

Are some people born with more courage than others? If we feel that we are the timid type, how can we "inflate our courage" so that we too can take bold, strong steps without melting into puddles of fear?

I love the story of Gideon in the book of Judges because it tells us so much about where true courage is born. Because the nation of Israel had been so disobedient, God is allowing the Midianites, a neighboring pagan nation, to conquer and enslave His people. Judges 6:6 says, "So Israel was brought very low because of Midian, and the sons of Israel cried to the Lord."

And God heard His people's cries for help, and He sent an angel to Gideon who was secretively pounding out some grain, hoping the Midianites wouldn't hear him.

The angel greeted Gideon as the young man cowered behind a cover of rocks, "The Lord is with you, O valiant warrior." It doesn't say that the angel had his tongue in his cheek, but given Gideon's fearfulness, it does seem like an exaggeration.

Soon we discover that the heavenly messenger is God Himself as we read, "And he [Gideon] said to Him, 'O Lord, how shall I deliver Israel?...But the Lord said to him, 'Surely I will be with you, and you shall defeat Midian as one man'" (Judges 6:15, 16).

There is so much more to this story, but it's not until Gideon stopped looking at his own lack of strength and rested in God's unlimited ability, that he was able to defeat the enemy—with only three hundred men and zero weapons.

One Christian writer wrote, "Courage is not the absence of fear. It is rather the capacity (or ability) to draw on the resources of God to do what we know we must do—respond in obedience to His call and in total dependence on His power."[20]

Can you think of a single reason why we should be controlled by fear? Doesn't it make sense that we should obey what Jesus asks us to do, knowing that God and all His heavenly host, stand ready to help us?

Our family has chosen a wonderful verse as the "beacon light" for our lives. Isaiah 41:10 says, "Do not fear, for I am with you; do not anxiously look about you, for I am your God. I will strengthen you, surely I will help you, surely I will uphold you with My righteous right hand."

# WHAT DO YOU THINK?

1. Why do you think the religious leaders of Israel lacked true courage?

2. When the angel of the Lord (actually it was the Lord Himself) appeared to Gideon, the young man answered, "O Lord, how shall I deliver Israel?" What was Gideon not seeing?

3. A Christian author wrote, "Courage is not the absence of _____. It is rather the capacity (or ability) to draw on the resources of _____ to do what we know we must do." Please fill in the blanks.

∞

# ANSWERS TO YOUR QUESTIONS

1. *They were trying to destroy the Son of God because they were jealous of Him. Jesus constantly exposed their hypocrisy and greed, and they wanted to remain in darkness. People who act out of pride and anger, usually lack the courage to stand firm in their decisions regardless of the consequences.*

2. *Gideon did not understand that God was not choosing him because he was strong and powerful. God delights in taking weak people like ourselves, and using us for His glory. The Lord was just looking for a willing servant. (See 2 Corinthians 12:9, 10).*

3. *The two words are: fear and God.*

*Sacrificial giving pleases God*

## 81. GIVING ALL YOU'VE GOT

*And He looked up and saw the rich putting their gifts into the treasury. And He saw a certain poor widow putting in two small copper coins. And He [Jesus] said, "Truly I say to you, this poor widow put in more than all of them;...but she out of her poverty put in all that she had to live on."*
*Luke 21:1-4*

When we look at the area of "giving" in the Bible, we soon realize that God is talking about a lot more than just putting some money in the offering plate on Sunday. We read over and over in God's Word that Jesus wants us to give Him our abilities, our experience, our energy, our time—yes, our whole lives, to accomplish His will in this world. After all, we are His "hands and feet" here on earth.

Let's examine first of all why the Lord even brought up the subject of the rich person's giving to the temple treasury compared with that of the poor widow. As with most principles Jesus taught, the lessons had to do with people's hearts—their motive for giving, their love for God, and their attitude toward other people.

In the parallel passage in the gospel of Mark, it says that Jesus sat down in front of the temple treasury and watched the various people put in their gifts (Mark 12:41-44). Jesus saw it as a teachable moment, so He called the Twelve. The Lord watched wealthy people putting large sums of money in the box and said, "…for they all put in out of their surplus." What He meant was that although the rich put in large amounts of money, it probably came out of a fund of "extra money" that was not a real sacrifice. No doubt they made a big show about their giving so all their neighbors could see how generous they were.

Why was the widow's gift so meaningful to Jesus? After all, it was only two copper coins that amounted to one penny. Again, it was her motive or heart attitude in giving to God's work. Mark writes, "…but she, out of her poverty, put in all she owned, all she had to live on" (Mark 12:44). Was God pleased now that the widow had no money for food and clothes? Of course not. It was such an act of love for God that moved this dear lady to give "everything"—

such an enormous step of faith. It demonstrated that she undoubtedly loved God with all her heart and was trusting her very life to Him. She knew her heavenly Father would take care of her earthly needs.

What is the lesson for us? Just as prayer, witnessing, baptism, the Lord's Supper, and reading God's Word are acts of faith and worship, so is giving a generous portion of our earthly wealth to God for Him to use as He desires.

Let's be like the widow!

[See also: Mark 12:41-44]

## WHAT DO YOU THINK?

1. As Jesus sat in the temple watching the treasury where the Jews left their gifts, He saw rich people leaving large gifts. Why didn't He praise them?

2. What good was the widow's gift of one cent toward God's work?

3. What would be the best way for you to decide how much to give to the Lord's work? What areas other than money can you and I give to please the Lord?

## ANSWERS TO YOUR QUESTIONS

1. *They were giving out of their "surplus" or extra money. Jesus didn't praise them because they were not giving out of sacrificial hearts.*

2. *What pleases God regarding "giving" is the heart attitude. He wants it to be an act of worship.*

3. *Ask God to show you how much to give. Your parents can be a big help here too. The Lord is also pleased when we give Him our time, our abilities, our experience, and especially our love.*

*Jesus is coming in great glory*

## 82. WHEN JESUS RETURNS A SECOND TIME

*"And then they will see the Son of Man coming in a cloud with power and great glory. But when these things begin to take place, straighten up and lift up your heads, because your redemption [salvation] is drawing near."*
*Luke 21:27, 28*

Prior to this day, Jesus has been teaching His disciples and the crowd following Him in three areas:
- That He is the Messiah, the beloved Son of God
- That He came to earth for the purpose of laying down His life for the sins of all mankind
- That the religious leaders of the day—the chief priests, scribes, Pharisees, and Sadducees—were hypocrites who pretended to follow God, but were full of pride, greed, and hatred.

Luke 21:7 records that with just a couple of days before His cruel death, someone in the crowd asks Jesus a question about the end of the world: "Teacher, when therefore will these things be? And what will be the sign when these things are about to take place?"

We hear a lot about Christ's *first coming* to earth, don't we? The Savior was born in Bethlehem to a poor family from Nazareth, and was welcomed into the world without any fanfare by a group of simple shepherds. The nation of Israel went on with its business as usual, unaware that God the Son had come to earth.

And now Jesus is giving the crowd in Jerusalem a taste of what His *Second Coming* will be like at the end of the world. He won't be coming to a dirty stable in Judea for a few witnesses to see, but will appear to the whole world "in a cloud with power and great glory."

Matthew reports it this way: "For the Son of Man is going to come in the glory of His Father with His angels; and will then recompense [judge] every man according to his deeds" (Matthew 16:27).

The apostle John adds these details, "Behold, He is coming with the clouds, and every eye will see Him, even those who pierced

Him; and all the tribes of the earth will mourn over Him" (Revelation 1:7). Undoubtedly those who mourn or weep will be those who never trusted in Christ when they had the opportunity.

According to Paul's letters to the Thessalonians, at a strategic moment of God's choosing, Jesus will come in the air and all Christians will be taken up to heaven to be with Him in what is called *the Rapture*. Life will go on as usual for unbelievers here on earth following this miraculous event, except that it will be a time of great torment and suffering for them.

When Jesus returns "in power and great glory," all believers will come with Him. He won't just come in the air, but will actually return to earth. How exciting!

[See also: Matthew 24:29-31; Mark 13:24-27]

## WHAT DO YOU THINK?

1. What were three areas that Jesus frequently taught the crowds during His time of ministry on earth?

2. What are some of the differences between Jesus' "first coming" and His "second coming" to earth?

3. Who will see Christ when He comes "in power and great glory"?

## ANSWERS TO YOUR QUESTIONS

1. *These three areas are:*
   - *That He is the Messiah, the beloved Son of God*
   - *That He came to earth for the purpose of laying down His life for the sins of all mankind*
   - *That the religious leaders of that day were hypocrites who pretended to follow God, but were full of pride, greed, and hatred*

2. *In Jesus' "first coming," He was born of a virgin in a stable in Bethlehem. The first guests after His birth were humble shepherds. After so many days, the family returned to their home in Nazareth. When Jesus comes directly to earth at His "second coming," every person on earth will see Him. He won't be a newborn baby, but He will be the mighty King of Kings, in power and glory. All Christians will come with Him.*

3. *Everyone on earth will see Jesus at the time of His second coming. Many will mourn or weep because it will be too late to trust in Him as Savior.*

*The privilege of having God's Word*

## 83. WITH PRIVILEGE COMES RESPONSIBILITY

*"Heaven and earth will pass away, but My words [the Bible] will not pass away."*
Luke 21:33

Did you know that you have a treasure in your home? In fact, you may have several similar treasures. I'm talking about the Bible—God's holy Word. About now you're maybe thinking, "I can see that the Bible is important, but how is it a treasure?"

First of all, it's not just another book. Our verse tells us that it is the only book that is *eternal*—it will last forever! The paper, print, and glue will break down one day, but the words are from the very heart of God and will never disappear. It's so important that Jesus Himself is called "the Word": "In the beginning was the Word [Jesus], and the Word was with God, and the Word was God. He [Jesus] was in the beginning with God" (John 1:1).

We are so privileged to have God's living Word in our hands. Hundreds of different language groups around the world have never heard of the Bible, and so they couldn't read it even if they wanted to.

But with *privilege* comes *responsibility*! Those who have God's Word are accountable to God to obey it. We also have the responsibility to take the Bible to those language groups without it, and translate it into their languages, so that they too can savor the sweet words of God's promises, and learn about His wonderful Son, Jesus.

What do you think of the statement, "With 'privilege' comes 'responsibility'"? Kirk Cousins is currently the senior quarterback for the Michigan State University Spartans football team. Kirk spoke recently at a Big Ten Conference "Kickoff Luncheon" for players, coaches, and the press. He first spoke at length about the privilege of being a college football player—to represent MSU, his family, the fans, and alumni. He then pointed out that this privilege carries with it a responsibility to be a role model for young boys who look up to college ball players. All the publicity does not entitle the players to be obnoxious, to look down on others, and even break the law. They are responsible to represent well the name on the *front* of their jerseys (MSU), and the name on the *back* (their family). Kirk goes one step further and sees the importance of being a testimony for Jesus Christ to all those with whom he comes in contact.

As we read earlier, you and I are highly privileged to have God's eternal Word in our hands. This privilege makes us responsible to share it with others, and even take it to those around the world who have never once heard of Jesus.

[See also: Isaiah 40:8; John 15:7; Colossians 3:16; 1 Peter 1:24]

## WHAT DO YOU THINK?

1. What makes the Bible different from every other book?

2. Please explain in your own words the principle, "With privilege comes responsibility."

3. What are two responsibilities we Christians have, that go along with the privilege of owning a Bible?

## ANSWERS TO YOUR QUESTIONS

1. *God's Word, the Bible, is different from every other book in that it is "eternal." Since the truths contained in the Bible are direct from God's heart, like God, they will last forever.*

2. *In every aspect of our lives, where we have the privilege of: a family, good food, nice home, education, friends, and good health, we have a responsibility to use it for God's glory, and not just to build ourselves up in the eyes of other people.*

3. *Many people consider it to be no big deal that they have God's eternal Word in their possession. It actually makes us responsible to obey the Scriptures, but also to give ourselves sacrificially to see that those who don't have the Bible in their language will one day have it like we do.*

*Jesus' final Passover on earth*

## 84. JESUS' LAST PASSOVER WITH HIS DISCIPLES

*Now the Feast of Unleavened Bread, which is called the Passover, was approaching. And the chief priests and the scribes were seeking how they might put Him to death; for they were afraid of the people.*
*Luke 22:1, 2*

Even today, two thousand years after Christ's death on the cross, this celebration is still very important to orthodox (traditional) Jewish families. Every year they observe this ancient custom with a Passover meal.

God first gave instructions for the Passover at the time that the Israelites were still slaves in Egypt. At that time He said to Moses, "Speak to all the congregation of Israel, saying, 'On the tenth of this month they are each one to take a lamb for themselves, according to their fathers' households, a lamb for each household...Your lamb shall be an unblemished male a year old; you may take it from the sheep or from the goats. And you shall keep it until the fourteenth day of the same month, then the whole assembly of the congregation of Israel is to kill it at twilight. Moreover, they shall take some of the blood and put it on the two doorposts and on the lintel (top cross-piece) of the houses in which they eat it. And they shall eat the flesh that same night, roasted with fire, and they shall eat it with unleavened bread and bitter herbs'" (Exodus 12:3, 5-8).

After that, the Jewish people celebrated the Passover every year to remember what had happened in Egypt. The firstborn children of Pharaoh and all the other Egyptians were killed by God. The people of Israel, who had been slaves to the Egyptians under cruel conditions, were set free and allowed to begin their forty-year trip to the Promised Land of Canaan.

On the first day of the weeklong Passover celebration in Jerusalem, Jesus sent Peter and John to arrange a room where He could spend this last feast with His beloved twelve disciples.

While they reclined at the table together, John describes an emotional scene where Jesus rose and washed the feet of each disciple (John 13:5-17). The Lord wanted each one present to understand that following His death, resurrection, and return to heaven, they would be the ones to carry on His ministry of sharing the Good News. They needed to have the same spirit and attitude of humility that He had—they were to be servants and not rulers.

Following this meaningful act of meekness by God the Son, He told them that He would not eat this Passover meal again until the end of the world when He would reign as king in the Kingdom of God. Jesus is the fulfillment of the Passover Lamb. As John said in John 1:29, "Behold, the Lamb of God who takes away the sin of the world!"

[See also: Matthew 26:1-5; Mark 14:1, 2; John 11:45-53]

## WHAT DO YOU THINK?

1. What were the Jewish people of Jesus' day remembering when they celebrated the Passover meal at the beginning of the Feast of Unleavened Bread?

2. What did Jesus do during the meal to demonstrate that He wanted His disciples to have the attitude of servants and not rulers, as they carried on His ministry after His death?

3. How was Jesus connected to the Passover lamb which was sacrificed by each Jewish family at this particular feast?

## ANSWERS TO YOUR QUESTIONS

1. *The Jewish people remembered when God worked miracles to free their ancestors who were living as slaves in Egypt. God instructed Moses to tell His people to take one lamb without blemishes per family, kill it, roast it, and eat it. They were to take its blood and paint their doorposts and lintels so the lives of their first-born would be spared. The Egyptians did not do that so their first-born died. As a result of Israel's obedience to God's instructions, Pharaoh let them go free. (See specific instructions in Exodus 12:3, 5-8)*

2. *Jesus rose from the table where they were eating, took off His robe, and washed the feet of each of the disciples. This is a task normally carried out by a hired servant. He was modeling how a servant would act for His disciples, and then He explained that He wanted them to have the attitude of servants toward other people, and not rulers, following His death.*

3. *The Passover lamb of Moses' day was killed; its blood "covered" them and spared them from death when it was painted on the doorposts and lintel. It was an act of obedience and faith when they trusted God's Word. Jesus is God's Lamb who was crucified and shed His precious blood. All those who believe in His sacrifice are spared from "eternal death." Their sins are not only "covered," but they are forgiven and forgotten by God.*

*From the Passover to the Lord's Supper*

## 85. THE INITIATION OF THE LORD'S SUPPER

*And when He [Jesus] had taken some bread and given thanks, He broke it, and gave it to them, saying, "This is [represents] My body which is given for you; do this in remembrance of Me." And in the same way He took the cup after they had eaten, saying, "This cup which is poured out for you is the new covenant [agreement] in My blood."*
*Luke 22:19, 20*

This particular Passover meal that Jesus celebrated with His disciples was unique for several reasons:
- It would be the last one they would share together until Jesus comes to earth again as King.
- Jesus identified Judas as the disciple who would betray Him.
- The Lord washed the disciples' feet as a display of humility and servanthood.
- Partway through the meal, Jesus initiated what we call today *the Lord's Supper* or *Communion*.

The disciples would have grown up observing the Passover, and I'm sure it was almost always done the same way—a meal of lamb, unleavened (without yeast) bread, and bitter herbs. Now Jesus is describing something very different. Instead of them remembering the children of Israel in Moses' day sacrificing a lamb, eating it, and then leaving Egypt, Jesus is asking them to remember something else—Himself.

The Old Covenant (Agreement) was the Law that God gave to Moses on Mount Sinai. Israel was required to obey not only the Ten Commandments, but many other laws as well. Because the Israelite people often broke these laws, they were required to bring bulls and goats to the tabernacle or temple where priests shed the blood of these animals, to *cover* the people's sins. Now a "one time sacrifice" was about to be made by the perfect Lamb of God, who is Jesus Christ.

God knew that even though Jesus offered Himself to the Jewish people as their king, they would not accept Him. And so it was planned by the heavenly Father, that His own precious Son would be the once-for-all time Passover Lamb. He would die and shed His blood only once. All those who trust in His sacrifice as total payment for their sin, have eternal life.

To demonstrate this New Covenant, Jesus took some bread, gave the Father thanks for it, broke it, and announced to His disciples that the bread was a symbol of His body which would soon be broken on the cross. Then they all ate the bread. Jesus then took the drink—which was most likely a mild wine—and explained that it represented (or was a symbol of) His blood, which would soon pour down His dear body. Then they drank it together.

What a privilege that we Christians today can still remember Christ's death for us, every time we have communion.

[See also: Matthew 26:26-30; Mark 14:22-26; John 13:1-38; 1 Corinthians 11:23-25]

# WHAT DO YOU THINK?

1. What were the unique facts about the Passover meal in today's lesson? (Maybe the entire family can remember all four points.)

2. Jesus was God's Passover Lamb. What was the main difference between the offering under the Old Covenant (the lamb that had to be killed every year by each family) and the offering under the New Covenant (Jesus' life given as a sacrifice for mankind's sin)?

3. Part way through the meal, Jesus initiated a New Covenant or Agreement. Explain what Jesus did and what it meant.

# ANSWERS TO YOUR QUESTIONS

1. *Refer to devotional for the list of four unique facts.*

2. *Under the Old Covenant, each family had to kill their own lamb and they had to do it every year. Jesus Christ, the Lamb of God, offered Himself* once, *with His death on the cross, to pay the sin debt of all mankind. (See Hebrews 10:10-14)*

3. *Jesus took a piece of bread, gave thanks to the Father for it, broke it (signifying His broken body on the cross), and gave it to the disciples to eat. Next, He took the drink (probably a mild form of wine) and gave it to His disciples to take a drink of it. The bread was a symbol or example of His body which within a few hours would be nailed to a Roman cross. The cup of drink represented His blood which would flow out of His body from a soldier's lance. Both the bread and the drink were to be consumed regularly in remembrance of Jesus and His death.*

*Being great is being a servant*

## 86. I'M THE GREATEST! OR AM I?

*And there arose also a dispute among them as to which one of them was regarded to be greatest. And He said to them, "The kings of the Gentiles lord it over them; and those who have authority over them are called 'Benefactors' [helpers]. But not so with you, but let him who is the greatest among you become as the youngest, and the leader as the servant."*

*Luke 22:24-26*

Cassius Clay exploded onto the world scene after winning a gold medal for boxing at the 1960 Summer Olympics in Rome, Italy. I can still remember seeing him when he arrived back in the USA. The young eighteen-year-old bounced down the steps from the plane, his gold medal swinging from his neck, into a mob of media people. Shortly thereafter, Clay turned professional and began to capture the imagination of people who normally had little interest in boxing.

In 1964, he joined the Nation of Islam and changed his name to Mohammed Ali. Soon Ali began to refer to himself as "the Greatest." He would grab the microphone from an interviewer, stare into the TV camera, and declare, "I am the greatest!" What made him entertaining was that you couldn't tell if he was joking with his bragging or deadly serious.

To a large extent, Ali backed up his bragging with results as he won the World Heavyweight Championship three times during his brilliant career. A diagnosis of Parkinson's disease in 1984 stamped a definite end to his illustrious career as a boxer and entertainer.[21]

One urban legend making the rounds about Ali relates to an airplane flight he was making. The flight attendant approached his seat and said to him, "Mr. Ali, you will have to put your seat belt on." The boxer responded, "Superman doesn't need a seat belt!" Without missing a beat, the flight attendant replied, "Superman doesn't need an airplane!"

In today's devotional, we hear the disciples arguing over who is the greatest. The Lord Jesus had just finished talking to them about being a servant to all, and even modeled servanthood by washing all their feet. No sooner was he done and the disciples began arguing, each one trying to prove that he was better than all the others. How sad Jesus must have felt. He had taught His disciples for three years; He was on the brink of being brutally killed for the sins of the world; and what was on the minds of His closest disciples? "I am the greatest!"

Does that same attitude ever show up in the family? Do you ever feel that you should be served dinner first at the table? Do you expect someone else to pick up your clothes on the floor of your bedroom (read "mom" here), because it's too much bother? Do you grumble when you are asked to take the garbage out? If you can figure out how to work a computer, could you also figure out how to run a washing machine?

There is only One who is the greatest—and He died on the cross like a servant to pay for our sins.

[See also: Matthew 18:1-5; Mark 9:33-37; Luke 9:46-48]

## WHAT DO YOU THINK?

1. Is it all right to proudly proclaim that you are the greatest, if you are number one in your particular field (for example, top of your school class or number one pick in the NFL draft)?

2. What seemed to be the main theme from what Jesus shared with His disciples during the Passover meal?

3. Can you think of an area in your own life where you demonstrate the same "I am the greatest" attitude as the disciples did—at school, in your home, with your friends? PARENTS: This could be a very delicate area, but also very meaningful and rewarding.

## ANSWERS TO YOUR QUESTIONS

1. *The best answer is, "How did Jesus act when He was on earth?" He was perfect and holy, besides being all-powerful, so He really was the greatest in every single category. But He didn't constantly brag about it. In Matthew 11:29, Jesus rightly claimed that He is "gentle and humble in heart." We ought to let God brag on us. After all, every good thing we have, we received from Him. (James 1:17)*

2. *It seems that Jesus wanted to impress on His disciples that He came into the world as a servant, prepared to be savagely killed for the eternal benefit of others. As they continued His work after His death, He wanted them to take the position of servants also and not proud leaders because they had been Jesus' disciples.*

3. *Personal opinion.*

*Jesus agonizes in prayer*

## 87. THE GARDEN OF SADNESS AND SLEEP

*And He [Jesus] came out and proceeded as was His custom to the Mount of Olives; and the disciples also followed Him. And when He arrived at the place, He said to them, "Pray that you may not enter into temptation."*

*Luke 22:39, 40*

The last act of this great eternal drama is ready to unfold. Jesus and His disciples have enjoyed each other's fellowship one last time before His death. Shortly after Judas rushes from the upper room, the Lord and His disciples make their way down the stairs, along the rutted trail to the Garden of Gethsemane on the Mount of Olives.

All that Jesus has told them in the past three years about the suffering and cruel death that await Him, is beginning to grip their deepest emotions. They are sick with grief and fear at the thought of losing their beloved friend and Messiah.

Once in the garden, Jesus has eight of the disciples sit down with the instruction, "Sit here until I have prayed." Then He leads Peter, James, and John (Mark 14:33) deeper into the garden. Jesus asks the three to "remain here and keep watch with Me" (Matthew 26:38), and then He proceeds on further.

The emotions of these next moments are difficult for us to fully grasp, even though Luke describes them clearly. God the Son, God the Father, and God the Holy Spirit have been together for all eternity past in perfect love and union. Now the beloved Son is about to carry the sins of the entire world—past and present—to the cross. For the first time ever, God the Father will have to turn away from His dear Son, because He cannot look on sin—even though it was *our sin* and not His own.

Matthew tells us that Jesus fell on His face and prayed, "My Father, if it is possible, let this cup [suffering, carrying the world's sin, and death] pass from Me…" (Matthew 26:39). The Lord Jesus knew there was no other way, but the heaviness of the responsibility weighed on Him terribly. And then He finished His prayer by saying, "Yet not as I will, but as You will." What devotion! What obedience! What love!

Luke the doctor writes, "And being in agony He was praying very fervently; and His sweat became like drops of blood, falling down upon the ground" (Luke 22:44). One Christian writer describes a rare condition called *hematidrosis* [he-ma-ti-dro-sis]. When a person is under extreme stress and pressure, tiny blood vessels can rupture into the sweat glands, and the person sweats a mixture of sweat and blood.[22] Oh what agony our Savior must have experienced at that moment!

After an angel came and strengthened Jesus, He returned to His three friends and disciples. What a disappointment it must have been to find them sleeping, overcome with exhaustion. The drama had only just begun!

[See also: Matthew 26:36-46; Mark 14:32-42; John 18:1]

## WHAT DO YOU THINK?

1. Jesus was deeply moved emotionally while He prayed in the garden. What seemed to be His primary request of His Father? How would His request be possible?

2. What did Jesus say that clearly demonstrates His relationship with His Father in heaven?

3. Imagine that you are one of the three disciples with Jesus. What would you have done differently, while Jesus was praying, given the same circumstances? PARENTS: This could be a very sensitive but meaningful discussion.

## ANSWERS TO YOUR QUESTIONS

1. *His primary request seemed to be, "If there is any other way to provide salvation for the world without all the shame, embarrassment, agony, and brutality—plus the separation from You—could we consider that? But I know there isn't, because I know what Your will is. Therefore, I am determined to go ahead with it, to obey You."*

2. *Jesus was one hundred percent committed to fulfilling His Father's plan. He said, "Yet not as I will, but as You will."*

3. *Personal opinion.*

## 88. BETRAYED WITH A KISS

*While He was still speaking, behold, a multitude came, and the one called Judas, one of the twelve [disciples], was preceding them; and he approached Jesus to kiss Him. But Jesus said to him, "Judas, are you betraying the Son of Man with a kiss?"*
Luke 22:47, 48

Before we consider Judas' actual betrayal of Jesus, let's get a little background on the man. The Bible doesn't give us a lot of detail on Judas Iscariot's life. Was he raised as a child of influential wealthy parents who gave him everything his little heart desired? Maybe Judas grew up in a dirt-poor family where his father rarely came home at night sober, and would beat the young lad just for being alive.

We first read about this complicated man in Matthew's gospel where the twelve disciples are listed and the final name is, "Judas Iscariot, the one who betrayed Him [Jesus]" (Matthew 10:4). As far as his family is concerned, we only know that his father's name was Simon Iscariot (John 6:71).

Even at the early stages of the Lord's ministry, He was letting the disciples know that one of them would betray Him. In John 6:70 Jesus asks the question, "Did I Myself not choose you, the twelve, and yet one of you is a devil [evil person]?" Despite the fact that Judas was an unbeliever, and allowed the devil to enter and control him (John 13:2), the Lord still chose him to be a disciple, and he was even the treasurer who carried the money purse for the group.

When it was almost time for the Passover, Judas left the Lord and the other eleven, and headed straight for the chief priests and officers where they discussed how to plan Jesus' betrayal. We read, "And they [chief priests] were glad, and agreed to give him money. And he consented, and began seeking a good opportunity to betray Him [Jesus] to them apart from the multitude" (Luke 22:5, 6).

It was a perfect time for Judas to act, with Jesus in the isolated Garden of Gethsemane. He alerted his group of "religious cutthroats," made up of chief priests, officers of the temple, and elders. What a picture of greed and betrayal as Judas picked out Jesus in the dark and approached Him. Luke 22:48 tells us the sad story: "But Jesus said to him, 'Judas, are you betraying the Son of Man with a kiss?'"

The Lord of all creation had shown nothing but love to Judas for the past three years, and now the son of Simon Iscariot was betraying the Son of God—for a measly thirty pieces of silver (Matthew 26:14, 15). When Judas kissed Jesus, the chief priests had their man. What would you imagine Jesus would say to greedy Judas, when He knew what had just happened? He did not become angry or accusatory, and He did not call on angels to help Him. He simply said, "*Friend*, do what you have come for" (Matthew 26:50). Jesus loved him right to the end.

[See also: Matthew 26:47-56; Mark 14:43-50; Luke 22:3-6; John 18:1-11]

## WHAT DO YOU THINK?

1. Do you think God the Father knew that Judas Iscariot would betray His Son, when He led Jesus to pick this shady character as one of the Twelve?

2. Since Satan entered Judas before he betrayed the Lord, should we blame the devil rather than Judas?

3. Describe in your own words Jesus' attitude toward Judas, when the betrayer pointed the Lord out to the religious leaders by kissing Him.

## ANSWERS TO YOUR QUESTIONS

1. *Of course God the Father knew, since He is omniscient (knows everything—past, present, and future). Why would He still go ahead and select Judas, knowing he would betray His beloved Son? Part of the reason would probably be that all prophecy in God's Word must be fulfilled, and we read, "Even my close friend, in whom I trusted, who ate my bread, has lifted up his heel against me" (Psalm 41:9; John 13:18).*

2. *We always have a choice, and Judas undoubtedly allowed Satan to enter him. He could have denied the devil entrance, which makes Judas solely responsible.*

3. *Jesus was always kind and gracious. He didn't react angrily, but simply said to Judas, "Friend, do what you have come for."*

*Peter denies Jesus and weeps*

## 89. WHEN THE BIG FISHERMAN CRIED

*And the Lord turned and looked at Peter. And Peter remembered the word of the Lord, how He had told him, "Before a cock [rooster] crows today, you will deny Me three times." And he [Peter] went out and wept bitterly.*
*Luke 22:61, 62*

Do you remember right after Jesus washed all His disciples' feet, that they began to argue over who was the greatest—maybe the toughest, smartest, fastest, and best fisherman as well? Most likely Peter was right in the middle of it.

The Lord knew what was going on in the hearts and minds of His disciples and for some reason singled out Peter. In a loving tone He addressed him, "Simon, Simon, behold, Satan has demanded permission to sift you (all you disciples) like wheat..." (Luke 22:31). Notice the devil had to ask God for permission to test all the disciples' faith with hard trials.

Then the Lord explained that He had already prayed for Peter, as the representative or leader of the disciples, that he would be strong in trusting God during the hard times that were coming, rather than strong in self-confidence. Peter would deny he ever knew Jesus, but then later would recognize his failure, and stand up as a strong witness for the Lord. He would even be able to strengthen and encourage his fellow disciples.

At this point, however, Simon Peter was still full of confidence in his own strength, and he was sure he would never deny Christ—he claimed he would go to prison or even die for his Lord.

Jesus, always graciously honest, had to tell him the truth—that before the rooster crowed that morning, Peter would deny knowing Him three times.

William MacDonald, an excellent Bible teacher, notes that Peter actually denied the Lord six times before the following people: a young woman (Matthew 26:69); another young woman (Matthew 26:71); the crowd nearby (Matthew 26:73); a man (Luke 22:58); another man (Luke 22:59); and a servant of the high priest (John 18:26).[23]

One of the most touching scenes in the Bible follows shortly after Peter's final denial of his Savior. Today's verse tells us simply, "The Lord *turned and looked at Peter*." What a look of loving kindness it must have been! And then Peter remembered what the Lord Jesus had told him. What could he do but weep uncontrollably? He had in fact denied with curses that he even knew Jesus—probably out of fear.

Is there any way that you and I can relate to or identify with what Peter had just gone through?

[See also: Matthew 26:34, 35, 57-75; Mark 14:29-31, 53, 54; Luke 22:31-34; John 13:36-38, 18:12-18, 25-27]

# WHAT DO YOU THINK?

1. PARENTS: It might be worth dwelling a little longer on the question at the end of the devotional, just to see if any of your children make a connection to any time at school or elsewhere, when they failed to stand up for the Lord. It's certainly not something you would want to draw out too long.

2. What does Peter's bold statement that he would rather be killed than deny Jesus, tell us about our evaluation of our own strength?

3. Why did Peter cry so bitterly when all the Lord did was look at him?

# ANSWERS TO YOUR QUESTIONS

*1. See note to "Parents" in question one above.*

*2. It tells us that we are often not good judges of our own hearts. Peter was so sure he would be strong and faithful to the Lord when confronted with a threatening situation. I'm sure he never dreamed he would deny Jesus Christ—and certainly not six times. (See Jeremiah 17:9)*

*3. Although Luke doesn't say, I can imagine that Jesus looked at Peter in a loving and kind way. He never even had to say anything, and the big fisherman realized what he had done. He had denied the Lord Jesus Christ.*

*Jesus is crucified between two criminals*

## 90. JESUS PRAYS FOR HIS PERSECUTORS

*And when they came to the place called The Skull, there they crucified Him and the criminals, one on the right and the other on the left. But Jesus was saying, "Father, forgive them; for they do not know what they are doing."*
Luke 23:33, 34

By this time, Jesus has already gone through unimaginable torture. The gospel of Matthew records the cruel mockery and brutal beating of the Savior. How humiliating for the Creator of the universe to be stripped down to His underclothes in front of a whole crowd of rough soldiers, and then be dressed in a make-believe royal robe. Can't you picture the laughing and cursing going on while Jesus humbly stands in silence?

A couple of soldiers think it would be a big joke to make this supposed King of the Jews a crown. They take some branches with thorns and carefully craft a crown, ramming it down on Jesus' head. The Lord winces in pain as the thorns puncture the skin causing blood to flow down over His face in narrow streams. Again the soldiers mock Him and pretend to bow down before Him, still continuing to curse.

Some soldier thinks the king should have a scepter, so he finds a reed (like a bulrush) and places it in the Lord's hand. Roughly he yanks it away again and beats Him on the head with it. Soldier after soldier spit in Jesus' face—that beautiful gracious face that smiles at children and welcomes the sick and needy. Another grabs a handful of beard and yanks it out by the roots.

We then read that Jesus is led to a place called "The Skull," also called Calvary (Latin name) and Golgotha (Aramaic name), and was crucified. Crucifixion was the cruelest means of death that the Romans could think of—reserved only for the worst non-Roman criminals. How strange that the kindest, most loving person to ever walk this earth would be killed this way! Jesus remained on the cross for roughly six hours (9:00 AM to 3:00 PM).

As Jesus hangs there on the cross—nailed by His hands and feet—the crowd notices His dry, blood encrusted lips moving. What is He saying? Is this King of the Jews cursing all of Israel for not accepting Him as their ruler? Is He spewing out hatred against the Romans who tried and punished Him illegally?

The soldiers, Jewish religious leaders, and mourners inch closer to His cross to try and make out His muffled words. Over and over they hear the same love-filled request, "Father, forgive them; for they do not know what they are doing."

How amazing! How gracious! How like the Son of God! Even while He is suffering the most extreme pain possible, His heart and mind think only of the eternal judgment His cruel tormentors will face before God. Instead of wanting His Father to increase their punishment, He wants only for them to be forgiven of their sin and have the opportunity to be added to God's family.

Hallelujah! What a Savior!

[See also: Matthew 27:32-56; Mark 15:21-41; John 19:17-30]

## WHAT DO YOU THINK?

1. What three names were given to the location outside of Jerusalem where Jesus was crucified?

2. Explain in your own words what Jesus was saying from the cross, in today's verses.

3. What does Jesus' choice of words tell us about His nature and personality?

## ANSWERS TO YOUR QUESTIONS

*1. Jesus was crucified at the place called "The Skull," Calvary (Latin name), and Golgotha (Aramaic name).*

*2. Personal opinion. Jesus was saying, "Father, forgive them; for they do not know what they are doing."*

*3. The fact that the Lord Jesus was not saying hateful, angry things, but rather was asking God the Father to forgive His persecutors because of their ignorance, demonstrates that His heart was full of love and mercy, even for His worst enemies.*

*Jesus converses with the criminals*

## 91. THE PROMISE OF PARADISE

*And one of the criminals who were hanged there was hurling abuse at Him, saying, "Are You not the Christ? Save Yourself and us!" But the other answered, and rebuking him said, "Do you not even fear God, since you are under the same sentence of condemnation?"...And he was saying, "Jesus, remember me when You come in Your kingdom!" And He [Jesus] said to him, "Truly I say to you, today you shall be with Me in Paradise."*
*Luke 23:39, 40, 42, 43*

Luke has recorded an amazing conversation between Jesus and the two criminals crucified along with Him. All three were in extreme agony with nails through their hands and feet, and yet they engaged in a discussion that gives us so much helpful information:

- Early on, both robbers were yelling insults at Jesus, similar to the chief priests, scribes, and elders. (Matthew 27:44)
- At some point, the one criminal stopped his abusive comments and had a change of heart and mind—he repented.
- This man's first action was to rebuke his partner in crime for his unkind words. What made the difference? Something about Jesus' attitude and gracious words convinced him that this truly was the long-awaited Jewish Messiah. As God the Son, He obviously did not deserve to be there. This criminal's confession of faith was clear in his words, "Do you not even fear God?"
- The repentant criminal now turns to Jesus and all he asks of the Savior is that he be "remembered" by Him when He comes in glory as King, at the end of the world. Obviously he had either heard Jesus' teaching firsthand, or been taught by someone else who knew the Scriptures.

And then we read these powerful words—the beloved Son of God's *second* saying from the cross. Not only will He "remember" this new believer in His future kingdom, but Jesus promises, "Truly I say to you, *today* you shall be with Me in Paradise." How that must have brought joy to the heart of this new child of God. The creator of the heavens and earth was declaring that this very day, he would be present with Him in heaven (called "paradise" here – See 2 Corinthians 12:2, 4).[24] Not only would the robber be in heaven, but he would be there *with Jesus*.

This story tells us so much, doesn't it? The main truth shines through all the gloom of Calvary that the worst of people can be saved by trusting in Jesus' death on the cross, as payment for their sin.

Salvation is clearly by faith in Christ's death, burial, and resurrection!

[See also: Matthew 27:44; Mark 15:32]

## WHAT DO YOU THINK?

1. What was so unusual about the location of the conversation between Jesus and the two criminals?

2. What appears to have caused the one robber to change his thinking and attitude toward Jesus?

3. What did Jesus say to the newly believing robber to indicate that to be saved, it's enough to simply trust in Jesus' death, burial, and resurrection as payment for his sin?

## ANSWERS TO YOUR QUESTIONS

1. *All three persons in the conversation were nailed to crosses and were in extreme pain, undoubtedly grossly dehydrated, and listening to verbal abuse shouted at them.*

2. *He must have had some prior knowledge that a Messiah was coming who one day would rule as the King of Kings. At some point, he believed that this gracious, kind man on the cross next to him was innocent of all sin, because He was God's Son. He repented of his sin and trusted in his new Savior. The Lord Jesus confirmed this criminal's salvation with a promise of eternal life.*

3. *On the basis of this robber's simple confession of faith—and nothing else—Jesus promised him that that very day they would both be in heaven together.*

*Christ's concern for His mother's future*

## 92. "BEHOLD YOUR MOTHER!"

*And all the multitudes who came together for this spectacle, when they observed what had happened, began to return, beating their breasts. And all His acquaintances and the women who accompanied Him from Galilee, were standing at a distance, seeing these things.*

*Luke 23:48, 49*

What a mix of emotions there must have been on that wretched hill called Golgotha—the place of The Skull. Crude Roman soldiers laughed at and mocked the Son of God as they gambled for His clothing.

The chief priests, scribes, and elders watched Jesus' painful death in moods of hate and jealousy. "Who does this uneducated Galilean think He is, calling Himself the Messiah—the Son of Man," they probably mumbled to each other.

Ordinary Jewish pilgrims traveling to the great city of Jerusalem for Passover, would stop for a moment, see the three forms writhing in pain on their individual wooden crosses, shake their heads in mock concern, and hurry on into the walled city below. They had a lot of celebrating to do.

Then there were Jesus' followers. Where were the Lord's disciples who He groomed and trained for this very day and beyond? Other than John, called the disciple whom Jesus loved, the disciples were nowhere to be found. Most likely they were hiding out in some relative's attic, waiting until all the brutality was over. Simon Peter, of course, was warming himself by a fire, hoping not to be identified.

Finally, there was a group of women who had followed Jesus approximately seventy miles from Galilee, in order to minister to and help their Lord and Master. Luke tells us that they were "standing at a distance, seeing these things."

Who were these women? John tells us there were four who were better known—Mary, the earthly mother of Jesus; His mother's sister Salome; Mary the wife of Cleopas; and Mary Magdalene (John 19:25). You would expect that Jesus would be totally focused on His own physical condition. But instead, through blood-crusted eyes, He saw Mary there, and in a kind and loving tone said, "Woman, behold, your son!" referring to John. And then He turned His thorn-crowned head toward John and said, "Behold, your mother!" This was His *third* saying (John 19:26, 27). Isn't it just like Jesus to be thinking of the future care of His earthly mother, even as He hung there paying the penalty for our sin?

[See also: Matthew 27:55, 56; Mark 15:40, 41; John 19:25-27]

## WHAT DO YOU THINK?

1. Who were some of the different classes of people there by Jesus' cross watching him die an agonizing death?

2. There were three "Marys" standing together at a distance, along with Salome, observing Jesus' crucifixion. Where were they from? Can you identify who they were?

3. What do Jesus' words to His disciple John and His mother indicate about His character and nature?

## ANSWERS TO YOUR QUESTIONS

1. *Roman soldiers, chief priests, scribes, elders, Jewish travelers on their way to Jerusalem for Passover, and Jesus' followers including the four women together.*

2. *The three "Marys" were: Mary, the earthly mother of Jesus; Mary, the wife of Cleopas; and Mary Magdalene. They had traveled from Galilee, about seventy miles away.*

3. *Even though Jesus was experiencing excruciating pain there on the cross, He was thinking about His mother's care and comfort after His death. This shows His kindness, thoughtfulness, and unselfishness.*

*The Father turns His back on Jesus*

## 93. WHY DID GOD THE FATHER FORSAKE HIS SON?

*And the people stood by, looking on. And even the rulers were sneering at Him, saying, "He saved others; let Him save Himself if this is the Christ of God, His Chosen One."*
*Luke 23:35*

As you and I read in the Gospels about what Jesus went through physically, we are horrified. How could the perfect Son of God ever be allowed to endure such pain, embarrassment, and betrayal? But there was so much more going on there on the cross that could be seen (the visible blood flowing down that precious body) or heard (the hoots and foul comments that crashed like waves upon His holy ears).

Jesus was carrying on His sinless being, the sin of the entire world for all time. Think of the thousands of times we have each sinned—anger, rebellion, lying, selfishness, and pride. Then, multiply that times the number of every human who ever lived and will live from Adam and Eve to the end of time. What an enormous and ugly mountain of ungodliness standing before the holiness and perfection of God.

And it all rested on the naked shoulders of our Savior as He hung there alone on the cross. Luke doesn't give us all the sayings of Christ at this time, so we have to turn to the other Gospels for a complete list. In Matthew 27:46, we read the question that Jesus already knew the answer to: "My God, My God, why [have You] forsaken Me?"

It's almost impossible for us to fully grasp the depth of emotional pain in Jesus' words. For all eternity past, God the Father, God the Son, and God the Holy Spirit—three persons, and yet one God—had enjoyed perfect love and union together. And in this moment of history, Jesus was carrying all our sin and receiving its punishment. God had to punish our sin because He is holy and just. Because of His love for us, the beloved Son was on the receiving end of all of the Father's righteous anger against our sin.

The physical pain must have been excruciating, but the separation and loneliness when the Father had to turn away from His dear Son, is far beyond our understanding.

Elizabeth Barrett Browning described the scene so well:
"Yea, once, Immanuel's orphaned cry
His universe hath shaken—
It went up single, echoless,
'My God, I am forsaken.'"[25]

Once again, we come face to face with the glorious truth that Jesus carried our sins to the cross with Him, and there on the place called Calvary, He paid the penalty for our sin. And what does He ask us in response? Only that we trust in His sacrifice for us and receive—for free—His everlasting gift.

[See also: Matthew 27:45, 46; Mark 15:33, 34]

## WHAT DO YOU THINK?

1. In addition to the physical pain that Jesus experienced there on the cross, what added to His suffering and torment?

2. Why did God the Father turn away from His beloved Son at the very moment that He needed His comfort the most?

3. Jesus carried all of mankind's horrible sin on His shoulders while He paid our sin debt that we were unable to pay ourselves. What does Jesus ask in return?

༺❦༻

## ANSWERS TO YOUR QUESTIONS

1. *As Matthew describes the scene in Jesus' own words, "My God, My God. Why have You forsaken Me?"*

2. *Because Jesus carried all of mankind's sin on Himself there on the cross, God the Father was forced to turn away from His dear Son. God is perfectly holy and without a single sin, and as such, could not look upon our sin. The Father's love for His Son never changed, but He could not have intimate fellowship with Jesus while He carried our sin.*

3. *Because Jesus' payment for our sin is a "free gift from God," there is nothing we can pay. He only asks us to believe or trust that Jesus paid our personal sin debt.*

*Jesus is offered a bitter drink*

## 94. THE BITTER DRINK

*And the soldiers also mocked Him, coming up to Him, offering Him sour wine, and saying, "If You are the King of the Jews, save Yourself!"*
*Luke 23:36, 37*

Can you think of a time when you were so thirsty for a drink of water that you would have traded anything you owned just for a large glass of ice water? Very few of us ever reach that point, but I've come close a few times.

When our family was going through the New Tribes Mission training program, we had a training exercise in the summer called "Jungle Camp." Each family had two weeks to build a house in the woods—a log frame covered with black plastic—and then live there for six weeks. Each house had to have beds, a stove (from a metal barrel), a shower, a table and chairs—and we can't forget central outhouses. We had to take enough food and supplies for 1½ months, because during this time, we weren't allowed to return to our apartments, even though they were only a few hundred yards away.

During this time, the men would go on a three day hike on the Bruce Trail in northern Ontario, Canada, carrying everything we needed in backpacks, including two-man pup tents. We would hike 10-12 miles per day on a marked forest trail carrying 50-60 pound packs on our backs. I have never been so thirsty in all my life.

I'm sure my thirst was nothing compared to what Jesus experienced there on the cross. Most likely He had not had anything to drink since He left the upper room with His disciples. He must have been seriously dehydrated, having experienced the loss of blood and severe sweating.

In Mark's gospel it's reported, "And they tried to give Him wine mixed with myrrh; but He did not take it" (Mark 15:23). Apparently the myrrh was a type of mild anesthetic to dull the pain, but Jesus did not choose the easy way.

Later, John reports Jesus' *fifth* saying: "After this, Jesus, knowing that all things had already been accomplished, in order that the Scripture might be fulfilled, said 'I am thirsty.' A jar full of sour wine was standing there; so they put a sponge full of the sour wine upon a branch of hyssop, and brought it up to His mouth" (John 19:28, 29). And then we read that He drank it.

How horrible! That the Son of God, creator of all things, should be given such a bitter mix to drink, is unthinkable! And why did He go through such agony? Because of the joy in His heart at being able to pay for my sin and yours—so that we would trust in Him and receive the free gift of salvation.

[See also: Matthew 27:34, 48; Mark 15:23, 36; John 19:28-30]

# WHAT DO YOU THINK?

1. Can you think of a time when you were so thirsty that you will probably never forget the incident?

2. What did the soldiers give Jesus to drink when He moaned that He was thirsty? [NOTE: There were two different occasions where something was offered to Jesus to drink.]

3. Why did Jesus, the all-powerful Son of God, not step down off the cross in a miraculous way to demonstrate to all those mocking Him that He really was the King of the Jews.

# ANSWERS TO YOUR QUESTIONS

1. *Personal opinion.*

2. *According to Mark's gospel, Jesus was offered wine mixed with myrrh, but He refused to drink it. John writes that just before His death, Jesus said that He was thirsty. He was given a sponge filled with sour wine and He drank some of the bitter liquid.*

3. *God's whole plan was that His Son Jesus—the holy Lamb of God—had to be sacrificed there on the cross as a perfect offering to pay for our sins. He had to shed His blood and die. If Jesus had come down from the cross—which He had the power to do—He would have been disobeying His Father's plan and our sin debt would not have been paid. We would still be lost in our sin and destined for hell.*

*Jesus' last breath*

## 95. "IT IS FINISHED!"

*And Jesus, crying out with a loud voice, said, "Father, into [Your] hands I commit My spirit." And having said this, He breathed His last.*

*Luke 23:46*

It's easy to look at today's verse that reports Jesus' *sixth* saying from the cross, and merely say, "Well, He finally died!" But there was so much more taking place at that moment.

The time of Jesus' death was 3:00 PM (the "ninth hour"), but there had been a thick darkness over all the land since noon (the "sixth hour"). The Bible does not mention any words from the lips of our Savior during this three-hour period of darkness (Luke 23:44). Some think this was most likely the time when our sin debt before God was paid for by the Lord Jesus. Satan had doubtless thought he had defeated God's beloved Son by brokering a corrupt agreement between Judas Iscariot and the chief priests.

Suddenly, a loud cry of victory pierces the thick darkness! In John 19:30, the Savior of mankind declared triumphantly, "It is finished!" What is finished? The payment for our sin has been *paid in full*! A single Greek word captures this glorious theme, declaring, "The work you gave me to do is completed" or, "God the Father's holy demand of a perfect sacrifice as payment for man's sin has been met" or, "There is no more offering needed for man's sin" or, "The Lamb of God has taken the place forever of the yearly Passover Lamb."

And then as a final act of submission to His heavenly Father, Jesus dismissed or "gave up His spirit" with the words of an obedient Son, "Father, into [Your] hands I commit My spirit." This was a "voluntary sacrifice" as Jesus' had willingly given His life for us. His final words were calm and deliberate with no indication of resentment toward His Father at all. He died knowing that the triune God's love for mankind was fulfilled through His shed blood.

One interesting fact to note is that the soldiers broke the legs of both criminals to quickly end their lives.[26] The Jews did not want these bodies defiling the land after dark (Deuteronomy 21:22, 23) especially on the Sabbath (Saturday). However, the soldiers did not break Jesus' legs, because He was already dead. This action fulfilled Old Testament Scripture which specifies that no bones of the Passover Lamb should be broken (Exodus 12:46; Psalm 34:20). Instead, a soldier thrust a spear into Jesus' side and bloody water flowed down that glorious body (John 19:34).

I'm sure your feelings and emotions are mixed as are mine, as you read Luke's account of our Savior's tortured death on Calvary's cross. Maybe now would be an excellent time to just bow your head and thank the risen Christ for His sacrifice. Because of Him, we will spend eternity in heaven in thankful praise of His kindness.

[See also: Matthew 27:50; Mark 15:37; John 19:30]

## WHAT DO YOU THINK?

1. Why did the soldiers break the legs of the two criminals crucified with Christ?

2. What does it mean that Jesus "gave up His spirit"?

3. Which of the following statements explain Jesus' last words, "It is finished!"
   - "The work You gave Me to do is completed."
   - God the Father's holy demand of a perfect sacrifice as payment for man's sin has been met.
   - There is no more offering needed for man's sin.
   - The Lamb of God has taken the place forever of the yearly Passover Lamb.

## ANSWERS TO YOUR QUESTIONS

1. *The soldiers broke the criminals' legs to end their lives, since under Jewish law there were not to be bodies hanging on a tree or cross after dark. They didn't break Jesus' legs because He was already dead.*

2. *Jesus voluntarily gave up His life as payment for our sin. He didn't accidentally die at the very last, but He willingly dismissed His spirit.*

3. *All of them.*

*Angels' instructions to grieving women*

## 96. WHEN THEY FORGOT TO REMEMBER

*...and as the women were terrified and bowed their faces to the ground, the men [two angels] said to them, "Why do you seek the living One among the dead? He is not here, but He has risen. Remember how He spoke to you while He was still in Galilee, saying that the Son of Man must be delivered into the hands of sinful men, and be crucified, and the third day rise again." And they remembered His words,...*
*Luke 24:5-8*

I have the hardest time remembering people's last names. I even try to concentrate while a stranger is telling me, and yet I'm usually doing well to come away with their first name. Even telling myself, "Next time I'm really going to concentrate," doesn't seem to help.

It's a little bit of comfort to realize that Jesus' disciples had good "forgetters" also. It's so obvious in this final chapter of Luke that the women and the Lord's other followers were not even considering the fact that their Messiah was going to come back to life after three days in the grave.

Mary Magdalene, Joanna, Mary the mother of James, and some other women arrived at Jesus' tomb carrying spices and expecting to prepare the Lord's body for burial. Their shock and surprise was partly because of the angels there who announced Jesus' resurrection, but a good deal of amazement had to be that there was no body there in the tomb.

Didn't the Lord tell all His disciples that He was going to be crucified and rise again in three days? Indeed He did! Luke wrote earlier, "And He [Jesus] took the twelve aside and said to them, 'Behold, we are going up to Jerusalem, and all things which are written through the prophets about the Son of Man will be accomplished. For He will be delivered to the Gentiles, and will be mocked and mistreated and spit upon, and after they have scourged Him, they will kill Him; *and the third day He will rise again*'" (Luke 18:31-33).

That seems pretty clear to me. In Matthew's gospel, he tells us that Peter obviously heard what Jesus said, because the big fisherman responded with, "...God forbid it, Lord! This shall never happen to You" (Matthew 16:22). Still, the Lord Jesus told His disciples plenty of times that the grave could not hold Him longer than three days, and He would come back to life.

So, where does that leave Jesus' followers? Once the angels asked the women, "Remember how He spoke to you…" today's verses tell us, "And they remembered His words…"

By the way, I wonder if there is a good method for remembering people's names.

[See also: Matthew 28:1-10; Mark 16:1-8; John 20:1-10]

## WHAT DO YOU THINK?

1. Who were the first people to come and visit Jesus' burial tomb, early in the morning following His death?

2. What are two reasons why the women were so amazed when they arrived at the tomb?

3. Have you ever forgotten to do something very important, when you were told very clearly what to do, when, and how?

## ANSWERS TO YOUR QUESTIONS

1. *Mary Magdalene, Joanna, Mary the mother of John, and some other women followers of Jesus, were the first ones to arrive at the tomb early in the morning.*
   *NOTE: In case, like me, you tend to get all "the Marys" mixed up, here is a list, thanks to one Bible commentator: Mary, the mother of Jesus; Mary, the mother of John Mark (Acts 12:12); Mary of Bethany (Luke 10:42); Mary, the mother of James and Joses, and wife of Clopas (John 19:25); and Mary Magdalene (Luke 8:2).*[27]

2. *First, they would be amazed to see two male angelic beings who apparently rolled the stone aside that covered the tomb opening. Second, the two men announced to them that Jesus' body was not inside the tomb because He had risen from the grave—just like He had said.*

3. *Personal opinion. It would be good to ask each child and parent to fortify the fact that we all forget at times.*

*Jesus teaches two forgetful disciples*

## 97. THE BIBLE IS "HIS-STORY"

*And He said to them [two of Jesus' disciples], "O foolish men and slow of heart to believe in all that the prophets have spoken! Was it not necessary for the Christ to suffer these things and to enter into His glory?" And beginning with Moses and with all the prophets, He explained to them the things concerning Himself in all the Scriptures.*

*Luke 24:25-27*

Can't you just picture Cleopas and his companion plodding along the seven mile trip from Jerusalem to their homes in Emmaus? They are heartsick with grief that their Lord and Master was crucified. The two had been so sure that He was the Messiah who would set them free from the bondage of Rome and establish His glorious kingdom on earth, but now He was dead.

As they share their disappointments, they suddenly hear footsteps behind them on the road, and turning around they see a stranger—one who is obviously ignorant of all that has been taking place in Jerusalem from the cross to the tomb. Jesus did not allow them to recognize Him.

In addition to reports from the other disciples, they had heard from "some women" that Jesus' body was nowhere to be found. I can hear Cleopas saying, "These ladies even said that angels told them the Lord was not there because He had risen alive from the dead—we sure don't need rumors like that getting started."

And then one of the greatest "Old Testament Survey" classes ever given took place, right there on the road to Emmaus.

First, Jesus lovingly rebuked His two followers who were overcome with disappointment. They were so taken up with the *glory* of Christ setting up His kingdom, that they couldn't understand that *suffering* had to come first.

And then we read today's wonderful verse how Jesus began with Genesis and followed through all the books of the Prophets, pointing out one common theme—Himself.

Does that seem strange to you? Are you wondering where the name Jesus Christ appears in the Old Testament? You won't find that sacred name there, but as one writer said, "The key to understanding the Bible is to see Jesus Christ on every page."[28] The Bible is *His-story* or a record of the person and work of the blessed Son of God.

Jesus must have started teaching Cleopas and his friend the creation story, and continued with God's promise of a savior to Abraham; the Passover Lamb; the sacrifices in the tabernacle and the temple; and the many Psalms that describe the Shepherd/Savior of mankind. Surely the Lord paused to explain in detail the meaning of Isaiah 53.

Can you even imagine what a thrill it would have been to be walking with the two disciples and the Lord Jesus, there on that dusty road to Emmaus? We can't ever do that, but we can thank God that we have the whole Bible in our language.

## WHAT DO YOU THINK?

1. Why were Cleopas and his companion so down in the dumps, as they walked to Emmaus?

2. What evidence did the two men have at this time that Jesus had actually risen from the dead?

3. What did Jesus do once the men got over explaining to Him why they were so discouraged?

༺❀༻

## ANSWERS TO YOUR QUESTIONS

1. *PARENTS: It might be good to read the whole story [Luke 24:13-35] to your children since the whole context helps to give the answer to this question.*

2. *Undoubtedly they had heard Jesus Himself teach that He would be crucified, but that on the third day He would arise from the grave. Also, they heard the testimony of the women who visited Christ's tomb and who heard the good news from the angels. Verse 24 says, "And some of those who were with us went to the tomb and found it just exactly as the women also had said..." These would be other disciples.*

3. *Jesus began to teach them from the Old Testament, pointing out that the entire Scripture has a single theme—the person and work of Jesus Christ. The Bible is "His-story"!*

*The risen Lord appears to His disciples*

## 98. A ROLLER COASTER OF EMOTIONS

*And when He had said this, He showed them His hands and His feet. And while they still could not believe it for joy and were marveling, He said to them, "Have you anything here to eat?" And they gave Him a piece of a broiled fish; and He took it and ate it before them.*
*Luke 24:40-43*

Where is your favorite roller coaster? The last one I was on had a particularly high hill, and I recall it crawling rather slowly up to the peak before it slammed down the other side. I knew the "rush" was coming, and the longer it took to reach the crest, the worse I felt.

We often hear people say that during an emotional time in their lives, they experienced a "roller coaster of emotions." Following Jesus' crucifixion, that's exactly what the disciples experienced. Here are a few of those emotions that Luke mentions in the last chapter of his gospel:

- SADNESS – (Verse 17) – When Jesus joined His two followers on the road to Emmaus, it says, "they stood still, looking sad." They were sure they'd never see their Lord again.
- HOPE – (Verse 21) – These disciples began to explain to Jesus why they were sad. They were hoping the Lord was the Messiah who would save Israel. Now they didn't know.
- AMAZEMENT – (Verse 22) – Cleopas and his friend must have talked to the women who went to Jesus' tomb, because they were amazed when the Lord's body wasn't there—and there were angels there too!
- UNBELIEF – (Verse 25) – When the two disciples finished telling Jesus about the recent events, the Lord rebuked them for being unwilling to admit that He had indeed risen from the grave as He had previously said.
- BURNING HEARTS – (Verse 32) – After Jesus had eaten with Cleopas and the others, He vanished from them. They now realized they had seen their Lord alive, and they discussed how

their hearts were warmed in His presence as He taught them from the Old Testament about Himself.
- SHOCK – (Verse 37) – Suddenly Jesus was in their midst again and they were startled. Even though He had a physical body, He was able to walk through walls—to appear and disappear.
- FEAR – (Verse 37) – Not only were Jesus' followers startled, but they were "plain old afraid." They knew it was the Lord, but they thought He was just a spirit.
- DOUBT – (Verse 38) – Since Jesus could see into their minds, He knew that His followers were still filled with doubts and questions, so He showed them the nail prints in His hands and feet.
- JOY – (Verse 41) – Can you imagine how thrilled they felt to realize that their Messiah was truly alive? They were excitedly happy—but how was it possible?

Can you imagine being there at that time and experiencing all those emotions?

[See also: Mark 16:14-18; John 20:19-23]

# WHAT DO YOU THINK?

1. Why were Cleopas and his friend sad when Jesus joined them on the road to Emmaus?

2. How do we know that the resurrected Son of God really did have a physical body and wasn't just a spirit?

3. When Cleopas and his friend thought back to Jesus' teaching on the Emmaus road about Himself, how did they describe the feeling in their hearts?

## ANSWERS TO YOUR QUESTIONS

1. *They thought for sure that Jesus was the Messiah they were waiting for. Now, it seemed that their Savior had been crucified and buried in a tomb. To make matters worse, they didn't know where His body was.*

2. *Jesus asked His followers for something to eat. They gave Him a piece of broiled fish and He ate it. Besides that, Jesus showed them the nail scars in His hands and feet.*

3. *They said that their hearts were burning within them while He taught them.*

*Jesus' Great Commission to all believers*

## 99. "PROCLAIMERS" TO THE WHOLE WORLD

*Then He opened their minds to understand the Scriptures, and He said to them, "Thus it is written, that the Christ should suffer and rise again from the dead the third day; and that repentance for forgiveness of sins should be proclaimed in His name to all the nations, beginning from Jerusalem. You are witnesses of these things."*
*Luke 24:45-48*

Many of the missionaries serving the Lord today are men and women who read the above verses, believed that Jesus was serious when He spoke them, and signed up to go to areas of the world where Christ's name had never been heard and the Bible didn't exist. Such was the case of one young family I'd like to tell you about.

As a young couple, they were full of enthusiasm to serve the Lord Jesus and grow to know Him more deeply. They had a young two-year-old daughter and were expecting their second child when they decided they had to get personally involved in fulfilling God's *"Great Commission."*

The more our couple heard veteran missionaries speak and the more they read books by Hudson Taylor and others, the more they realized that the "Go" in Matthew 28:19, and the "…and you shall be My witnesses…" in Acts 1:8, referred to *all* believers, and not just some special group of Christians.

One day, while the husband was getting ready for work, he reasoned, "This company that I work for is not going to last forever—in fact, it could easily disappear next week. I only have 'one life'; one opportunity to invest it fully for Christ."

The young couple prayed and discussed the matter for a number of months until their hearts were fully together, and then they applied to New Tribes Mission. Word came back from NTM that they were accepted for missionary training, and so the husband resigned his job—with a little fear and a lot of excitement.

Parents and friends were advised of what the young couple would be doing in the coming years—some were opposed to this step of faith while others rejoiced.

In September of 1969, this little family of four (the new baby girl was two weeks old) headed off to missionary training with their life savings of six hundred dollars, and ten dollars promised support from their home church.

When God asks His children to do something, He takes the responsibility to pay the bill. As the family went through the training, they experienced this principle first hand as the Lord supplied all their needs through a variety of sources.

The years rolled by, and God used this couple in NTM to: train missionaries; teach God's Word; live and work in Latin America; and serve in NTM leadership. The three children grew up to love the Lord Jesus, and established Christian homes of their own.

By now you've probably figured out that this brief history belongs to the author, his wife, and three children. We stepped out by faith forty-two years ago, believing that Jesus meant *us* when He said, "…all authority has been given to Me in heaven and on earth. Go therefore and make disciples of all nations…"

[See also: Matthew 28:18-20]

## WHAT DO YOU THINK?

1. Explain in your own words what Jesus is telling His disciples in today's verses.

2. "When God asks His children to do something, He takes the responsibility to_____."

3. At the end of today's devotional, we read some verses from the end of Matthew's gospel. What promise did Jesus make to His children who go into all the world with the Gospel?

## ANSWERS TO YOUR QUESTIONS

*1. Personal opinion. You might want to have all your children contribute to this answer.*

*2. "...He takes the responsibility to pay the bill."*

*3. Jesus promised, "...and lo, I am with you always, even to the end of the age."*

*The Lord returns to His Father*

## 100. WHEN JESUS RETURNED TO HEAVEN.

*And He led them out as far as Bethany, and He lifted up His hands and blessed them. And it came about that while He was blessing them, He parted from them. And they returned to Jerusalem with great joy, and were continually in the temple, praising God.*
*Luke 24:50-53*

You remember that the beloved Physician wrote both the gospel of Luke and the book of Acts. In the last few verses of his gospel, Dr. Luke tells us simply that the resurrected Jesus walked with His disciples out from Jerusalem to the town of Bethany on the eastern slopes of Mount Olivet. The Lord had often stayed there with His friends Lazarus, Martha, and Mary.

It was now over a month since Jesus had risen from the dead. What was He doing during this time? We read, "To these [eleven apostles] He also presented Himself alive, after His suffering, by many convincing proofs, appearing to them over a period of forty days, and speaking of the things concerning the kingdom of God" (Acts 1:3). He was teaching them!

What a picture that must have been—Jesus, surrounded by His eleven apostles—hugging this one, squeezing that one's shoulder, and giving a final word of comfort to others.

As He began to address the whole group, they must have stopped their chatter and listened carefully to every word. The Son of God was about to share His final words with them before returning to heaven. Lovingly He told them that they should stay right there in Jerusalem for "the Father's promise." Rather than heading right out to the ends of the earth to share Christ's gospel they needed God's "spiritual power." Winning souls is a divine work rather than something we can accomplish in our own strength. We can't argue people into heaven!

That power would be in the form of the Holy Spirit. Instead of Jesus being with His disciples day after day, like He had for the past three years, they would have God the Holy Spirit right inside each one of them to guide and empower them. Jesus continued, "...for John baptized with water, but you shall be baptized with the Holy Spirit not many days from now" (Acts 1:5).

The Lord's very last words, the sentences He wanted to leave ringing in their ears, were, "...but you shall receive power when the Holy Spirit has come upon you; and you shall be My witnesses both [at the same time] in Jerusalem, and in all Judea and Samaria, and even to the remotest part of the earth" (Acts 1:8).

Luke concludes by saying that Jesus raised His hands, blessed the group, and ascended into heaven, disappearing into the clouds. Other verses tell us that He went directly into God the Father's presence to sit down at His right hand. (Romans 8:34; Ephesians 1:20; Colossians 3:1). What a glorious reunion that must have been!

We have another promise from God—that His beloved Son Jesus is coming again one day to gather all of His saved ones to be in His loving presence forever. What a thrilling day that will be! EVEN SO COME BACK LORD JESUS!

[See also: Matthew 28:16-20; Mark 16:14-20; Acts 1:1-11]

## WHAT DO YOU THINK?

1. Why did Jesus tell the apostles that once He returned to heaven, they should wait in Jerusalem before going out to the ends of the earth?

2. Explain in your own words what Jesus' very last words were, that He wanted to leave ringing in His disciples' ears.

3. What thrilling event do we who know Jesus Christ as our personal Savior have to look forward to?

## ANSWERS TO YOUR QUESTIONS

1. *The apostles were to wait in Jerusalem "for what the Father had promised" (Acts 1:4). The promise was God the Holy Spirit, who would enter into each one of them and give them the spiritual power and guidance to win souls for Christ.*

2. *Personal opinion. The answer should relate to Acts 1:8.*

3. *Jesus is coming back to earth one day to gather together all those who have placed their trust in His death, burial, and resurrection, in payment for their sins. He will then take us to heaven to be with Him, where we will enjoy His loving presence forever.*

# THEME INDEX

| THEME | DEVOTION NUMBER |
|---|---|
| Abraham's bosom versus hell | 63 |
| A disciple takes up his cross | 34 |
| A neighbor cares for others | 38 |
| Angels' instructions to grieving women | 96 |
| A wrong choice can be deadly | 62 |
| Bearing spiritual fruit | 23 |
| Being great is being a servant | 86 |
| Believers are precious to God | 46 |
| Celebrating the wanderer's return | 58 |
| Christ loves to forgive sins | 29 |
| Christ's busy days before His death | 77 |
| Christ's concern for His mother's future | 92 |
| Criticism | 22 |
| Dependence on God | 21 |
| Don't worry about your next meal! | 48 |
| Everyone is my neighbor | 37 |
| Evil spirits | 16 |
| Faith in God's Word pleases Him | 30 |
| Family historian | 1 |

| | |
|---|---|
| First the suffering, then the glory | 67 |
| Five different baptisms | 12 |
| Following Jesus | 19 |
| Forgiving like Jesus forgave | 65 |
| From the Passover to the Lord's Supper | 85 |
| God is honest, but not fair | 47 |
| God never quits searching | 57 |
| Healed by faith | 18 |
| Hell and what it's like | 64 |
| Humility and pride | 11 |
| Humility is putting yourself last | 53 |
| If Pharisees were in charge | 5 |
| Investing in being a steward | 61 |
| Itching ears | 15 |
| It's the inside that matters | 44 |
| Jealousy instead of joy | 60 |
| Jesus agonizes in prayer | 87 |
| Jesus always did the Father's will | 72 |
| Jesus, a maturing young man | 8 |
| Jesus came to save sinners | 20 |
| Jesus can heal any disease | 32 |

| | |
|---|---|
| Jesus compares Himself to Jonah | 42 |
| Jesus converses with the criminals | 91 |
| Jesus' courage and the Pharisees' cowardice | 80 |
| Jesus cries over the people of Jerusalem | 76 |
| Jesus is crucified between two criminals | 90 |
| Jesus doesn't want anyone to perish | 73 |
| Jesus' final Passover on earth | 84 |
| Jesus' Great Commission to all believers | 99 |
| Jesus is always the same | 45 |
| Jesus is coming in great glory | 82 |
| Jesus is offered a bitter drink | 94 |
| Jesus is the "Expected One" | 27 |
| Jesus is worthy of praise and glory | 75 |
| Jesus knew He had to die | 49 |
| Jesus' last breath | 95 |
| Jesus' "boss" was His Father | 78 |
| Jesus longs for people's salvation | 52 |
| Jesus must be first | 36 |
| Jesus officially enters Jerusalem | 74 |
| Jesus returns to Nazareth | 14 |
| Jesus teaches two forgetful disciples | 97 |

| | |
|---|---|
| Jesus wants us to pray constantly | 41 |
| John's baptism | 10 |
| Judas' betrayal of Jesus | 88 |
| Learning to trust Jesus | 17 |
| Mary's surprise visitor | 3 |
| No need for fear | 4 |
| Nothing's too hard for Jesus | 33 |
| Our eyes shine out and see in | 43 |
| Peter denies Jesus and weeps | 89 |
| Pray continually! | 69 |
| Preparing the way for Jesus | 2 |
| Pride leads to delaying | 51 |
| Religious leaders plot Jesus' death | 79 |
| Repentance | 9 |
| Repentance involves worshiping Jesus | 28 |
| Sacrificial giving pleases God | 81 |
| Simeon, a faithful man | 6 |
| Temptation of Jesus | 13 |
| The best thing of all | 71 |
| The Father turns His back on Jesus | 93 |
| The importance of planning | 55 |

| | |
|---|---|
| The joy of returning to Christ | 59 |
| The Lord returns to His Father | 100 |
| The narrow door to salvation | 50 |
| The privilege of having God's Word | 83 |
| There's only one Number 1 | 35 |
| The risen Lord appears to His disciples | 98 |
| The simplicity of a humble man | 70 |
| Trust Jesus even in danger! | 31 |
| Two little words—thank you! | 66 |
| Walking the walk with Jesus | 24 |
| We need to be full of the Lord | 68 |
| What did Jesus mean by 'hate'? | 54 |
| What good is salt without flavor? | 56 |
| What is most important of all? | 40 |
| When Jesus was amazed | 26 |
| When Jesus was lost | 7 |
| Why are you so uptight? | 39 |
| Worthy of Christ's love? | 25 |

# NOTES

1. William MacDonald, *Believer's Bible Commentary, New Testament* (Nashville, TN: Thomas Nelson Publishers, 1990), 198.

2. Dr. Paul Brand and Philip Yancey, *Pain – The Gift Nobody Wants* (New York, NY: Harper Collins Publishers, Inc., 1993).

3. C. S. Lewis, *The Silver Chair* (New York, NY: Harper Collins Publishers, 1953).

4. Mark Buchanan, *Your God is Too Safe* (Sisters, OR: Multnomah Books, 2001), 47.

5. Warren W. Wiersbe, *The Bible Exposition Commentary, Volume 1* (Wheaton, IL: Victor Books, 1989), 200.

6. William MacDonald, *Believer's Bible Commentary, New Testament* (Nashville, TN: Thomas Nelson Publishers, 1990), 231.

7. Merrill F. Unger, *Unger's Bible Dictionary* (Chicago, IL: Moody Press, 1957), 509.

8. Wikipedia, *March of the Penguins,* directed and co-written by Luc Jacquet; co-produced by Bonne Pioche and the National Geographic Society, 2005.

9. Warren W. Wiersbe, *The Bible Exposition Commentary, Volume 1* (Wheaton, IL: Victor Books, 1989), 232.

10. Wikipedia, *The A-Team,* NBC Television Series, January 23, 1983 - March 8, 1987, Universal Television in association with Stephen J. Cannell Productions.

11. Warren W. Wiersbe, *The Bible Exposition Commentary, Volume 1* (Wheaton, IL: Victor Books, 1989), 237.

12. Wikipedia, *Jim Marshall, American football.*

13. www.fact-index.com, *Scrooge McDuck,* A cartoon character created by Carl Banks in 1947, and licensed by The Walt Disney Corporation.

14. John Walvoord and Roy B. Zuck, Editors, *The Bible Knowledge Commentary – New Testament* (Wheaton, IL: Victor Books, 1983), 247.

15. Wikipedia, C. S. Lewis, *The Screwtape Letters*, C. S. Lewis Pte. Ltd., Copyright 1942, 1996.

16. Mark Buchanan, *Your God is Too Safe* (Sisters, OR: Multnomah, 2001), 247.

17. Wikipedia, *1954 Cotton Bowl Game*.

18. Ravi Zacharias, A Slice of Infinity, Slice # 2510, *From Disparate Threads,* Ravi Zacharias International Ministries (RZIM).

19. Information courtesy of ABC News.

20. David Roper, *A Man to Match the Mountain* (Nashville, TN: Discovery House Publishers / Thomas Nelson, 1996), 39.

21. Wikipedia, *Mohammed Ali.*

22. Warren W. Wiersbe, *The Bible Exposition Commentary, Volume 1* (Wheaton, IL: Victor Books, 1989), 269.

23. William MacDonald, *Believer's Bible Commentary, New Testament* (Nashville, TN: Thomas Nelson Publishers, 1990), 267.

24. William Hendriksen, *New Testament Commentary, Luke* (Grand Rapids, MI: Baker Book House, 2002), 1033.

25. William MacDonald, *Believer's Bible Commentary, New Testament* (Nashville, TN: Thomas Nelson Publishers, 1990), 125.

26. John Walvoord and Roy B. Zuck, Editors, *The Bible Knowledge Commentary – New Testament* (Wheaton, IL: Victor Books, 1983), 340.

27. William Hendriksen, *New Testament Commentary, Luke* (Grand Rapids, MI: Baker Book House, 2002), 84.

28. Warren W. Wiersbe, *The Bible Exposition Commentary, Volume 1* (Wheaton, IL: Victor Books, 1989), 279.

# GLOSSARY

1. **Abraham's Bosom** – (16:22) – The Jews believed this was a place of eternal joy after death for the righteous, where Abraham resided. It's most likely another name for heaven.

2. **Altar of Incense** – (1:11) – A small wooden table overlaid with gold where incense was burned in the temple. It was placed in front of the veil leading to the Holy of Holies.

3. **Apostle** – (6:13) – Literally means 'one sent on a mission by an authority.' Jesus' twelve disciples were also called apostles. Matthias replaced Judas. Paul was the last apostle.

4. **Beelzebul** – (11:15) – The name came from a Philistine god, Baal, who was thought to be 'lord of the demons.' To the Jews, it was another name for Satan.

5. **Benefactors** – (22:25) – It was a title i.e. well doer, given to Gentile kings who claimed to be kind to their subjects, but were often cruel.

6. **Centurion** – (7:2) – He was an officer in the Roman army commanding one hundred men. Most of the centurions found in the New Testament, were men of good character.

7. **Council** – (22:66) – In Luke's gospel, the council was the Sanhedrin or Jewish Supreme Court.

8. **Cubit** – (12:25) – A Hebrew unit of measure from the point of the elbow to the tip of the middle finger—approximately eighteen inches.

9. **Denarius** – (20:24) – A small, silver, Roman coin that would commonly be wages for one day's work. It bore a picture of the ruling Caesar on one side.

10. **Disciple** – (5:30) – One who is a learner and follower of another i.e. Jesus, John the Baptist, and the Pharisees. Jesus' Twelve were chosen from the larger crowd of disciples.

11. **Doctors of the Law** – (5:17) – They were teachers of the Mosaic Law, usually from among the Pharisees, who received voluntary gifts rather than a salary.

12. **Dropsy** – (14:2) – Excess fluid accumulating in the body tissues due to organ failure. Edema is a more modern term.

13. **Elders** – (22:66) – These were influential men in each town and city of Israel. In Jerusalem they were lay workers in the Sanhedrin.

14. **Fasting** – (2:37) – The only fast in the Law of Moses was on the Day of Atonement. The Pharisees fasted—doing without food for 24 hours twice a week—to look religious before others.

15. **Feast of the Passover** – (2:41) – A yearly one-day celebration held in Jerusalem where Jews observed Israel's deliverance from bondage in Egypt.

16. **Hades** – (16:23) – It seems to be a temporary place of suffering in torment and flame where the unsaved go after death to await the Great White Throne Judgment of Christ.

17. **Kingdom of God** – (4:43) – God's kingship or rule in human hearts that results in salvation. It's a spiritual kingdom over which Christ will physically reign at the end of the world.

18. **Leaven** – (12:1) – Many believe that leaven (yeast) in the New Testament symbolizes evil i.e. hypocrisy. Just as leaven spreads through dough, so does evil spread through people.

19. **Leprosy** – (5:12) – A bacterial infection (also called Hansen's disease) that destroys the nerves especially of the hands and feet. In the Old Testament, lepers were considered 'unclean.'

20. **Levite** – (10:32) – Levi (one of Jacob's 12 sons), and his sons were set apart by God for serving in the Old Testament tabernacle. They assisted the priests in the Jerusalem temple.

21. **Mammon** – (16:9) – It refers to wealth and riches. Jesus taught that a believer's wealth should serve him or her to do God's will. Christians cannot love God and their belongings equally.

22. **Mina** – (19:13) – A Greek coin worth one hundred drachmas (one drachma was a laborer's daily wage) or approximately three month's wages.

23. **Palsy** – (5:18) – A weakness or paralysis of muscles over which a person normally has no control.

24. **Pharisee** – (5:17) – A small religious sect of Jesus' day that held to the letter of the Mosaic Law. They shunned the poor, the sick, the sinner, and the Gentile. They believed in the resurrection.

25. **Priest** – (1:5) – Twice a year, each of the 24 divisions of priests (descendants of Aaron) was on duty in the Jerusalem temple for one week. They could only burn incense once in a lifetime.

26. **Prophet** – (1:70) – God put His words in the mouths of these godly people, both to speak to His people Israel and to write Scripture for all people for all times. Many spoke of the Messiah.

27. **Publican** – (5:27) – These Roman appointees were located in all provinces of the Roman Empire where they collected taxes on almost everything. They were hated by the Jews.

28. **Repentance** – (3:8) – Literally means 'to change one's mind and attitude,' usually about one's sin. It doesn't mean the same as 'to feel sorry,' but Godly sorrow leads to repentance (2 Cor. 7:10).

29. **Sabbath** – (6:1) – The seventh day of the week (Saturday) was instituted by God in the Old Testament for Israel as a day of rest and worship. The first Sabbath was God's day of rest.

30. **Sadducee** – (20:27) – In Jesus' day, they were a religious party of wealthy families who controlled the temple. They did not believe in the resurrection of the body, eternal judgment, or angels.

31. **Scribe** – (5:30) – Religious Jewish men, mostly Pharisees, studied and taught the Law. Jesus called them hypocrites.

32. **Sepulchre** – (11:47) – It was a burial place or tomb, often carved out of a cave that would hold up to eight bodies. The entrance was covered with a large stone or door.

33. **Showbread** – (6:4) – Twelve loaves of bread made of fine (unleavened) wheat flour, placed on a table in the tabernacle in front of the veil into the Holy of Holies, and eaten by the priests.

34. **Son of Man** – (6:5) – A name used only by Jesus for Himself. It refers to His heavenly authority and power as God, as well as His humility and humanity.

35. **Steward** – (16:1) – A manager or overseer of a household, usually a servant or slave. They would also teach other slaves and the family's children. Christians are stewards of the Gospel.

36. **Synagogue** – (6:6) – A local Jewish building for worship, prayer, and the reading of Scripture. Built in towns throughout Israel, they became centers of religious and social life.

37. **Tetrarch** – (3:1) – The governor of one-quarter of a country. In New Testament Bible times, King Herod divided his kingdom among his four sons, each one being a tetrarch.

38. **Three tabernacles** – (9:33) – Peter was so awestruck at seeing Jesus transfigured in all His glory that he wanted to build three 'sacred tents' as memorials of this divine event.

39. **Unclean spirit** – (4:33) – Also called 'demons.' God created them as angels and they were once good. However they sinned and became agents of Satan doing evil in the world.

40. **Votive gifts** – (21:5) – Expensive gifts given by wealthy people for the Jerusalem temple. Herod the Great donated huge golden vines for above the entrance of the Holy Place.

# REFERENCES

1. William MacDonald, *Believer's Bible Commentary* (Nashville, TN: Thomas Nelson Publishers, 1990).

2. Merrill F. Unger, *Unger's Bible Dictionary* (Chicago, IL: Moody Press, 1957).

3. John F. Walvoord and Roy B. Zuck, Editors, *The Bible Knowledge Commentary – New Testament* (Wheaton, IL: Victor Books, 1983).

4. Warren W. Wiersbe, *The Bible Exposition Commentary – Vol. 1* (Wheaton, IL: Victor Books, 1989).

5. Everett F. Harrison, Editor, *The Wycliffe Bible Commentary* (Chicago, IL: Moody Press, 1962).

6. Charles C. Ryrie, *Basic Theology* (Chicago, IL: Moody Press, 1999).

7. Everett F. Harrison, Editor, *Baker's Dictionary of Theology* (Grand Rapids, MI: Baker Book House, 1966).

8. William Hendriksen, *New Testament Commentary – Luke* (Grand Rapids, MI: Baker Book House, 2002).

9. *Webster's New World College Dictionary, 4$^{th}$ Edition* (Cleveland, OH: Wiley Publishing, Inc., 2004).

10. Millard J. Erickson, *Christian Theology, 2$^{nd}$ Edition* (Grand Rapids, MI: Baker Books, 1998).

# ACKNOWLEDGEMENTS

Writing a book is a team effort! I might even go so far as to say that if an author insists on doing every aspect himself of putting a book together, he is missing the excellence that qualified partners bring. Someone said, "Teamwork is the ability to work together toward a common vision...It is the fuel that allows common people to attain uncommon results." I've had the privilege of working with some uncommonly talented people in my years with New Tribes Mission. Some worked directly on this project with me—many had indirect creative and spiritual impact on me simply by being every day coworkers.

A great deal of thanks goes to Carol Kaptain, editor extraordinaire, who applied her years of experience as a Bible translation consultant, to this project.

It's great to have a buddy like Jon Frazier to go to with printing questions.

Andy Daniels deserves considerable credit for formatting my rough product into a "real book."

I'm thankful for those who "family tested" my first book in this series, *Growing a Wise Family*, and gave me feedback.

Stacy Edwards www.designbystacy.com is a gifted graphic artist and I'm thankful for her cover designs.

I especially appreciate Dr. Gary Gilley, author and pastor of Southern View Chapel, Springfield, IL for writing the Foreword.

Thanks to those of you who reviewed draft copies of the text:
- Brad Stephenson – Lead Pastor, Deltona Alliance Church, Deltona, FL
- Dr. Laura Mae Gardner – International Personnel Consultant and Trainer, Wycliffe International & SIL, Orlando, FL
- Dr. Kit Flowers – Executive Director, Christian Veterinary Mission, Seattle, WA
- Ruth Ann Graybill – Therapist/Clinical Social Worker, Biola Counseling Center, Biola University, La Mirada, CA
- Perry Bradford – Executive Director, Barnabas International, Rockford, IL
- Michael Sullivan – Director of Church Relations, NTM-USA Executive Board, Sanford, FL

- Joe Dabrowski – Lead Pastor, First Baptist Church of Okemos, Okemos, MI
- Brian Esau – President & CEO, Red River Mutual Insurance Company, Steinbach, Manitoba, CANADA
- Joseph Goodman – Director of Personnel, NTM-USA, Sanford, FL

My dear wife Del is my sounding board, partner, and 'director of common sense.'

May this book abound to the glory of my awesome Savior Jesus Christ who is the greatest encourager of all.

DEAR READER........

Thank you for studying through these 100 devotionals from the gospel of Luke.

Our passion at Spring Glen Publishing is to encourage families to have a daily time together where Jesus Christ is glorified through prayer, Bible reading, quality conversation, edifying books, and even singing choruses.

We would be thrilled if you would let us know if you have any questions, suggestions, comments, or creative ideas you've discovered that would make these devotionals even more meaningful. And the bottom line is—did your children enjoy them?

Please contact us at:

>SPRING GLEN PUBLISHING,
>Box 530751,
>Debary, FL    32753-0751
>
>Tel. 386-668-1569
>
>Email – *bryan@ComeRestWithMe.com*
>
>Web – *www.SpringGlenPublishing.com*
>
>Blog – *www.ComeRestWithMe.blogspot.com*

BOOK ORDERS: If you would like to order copies, signed or unsigned, please contact us at the address above or by Email. There are SPECIAL DISCOUNTS on the purchase of multiple copies for Bible study groups, classes, and gifts.

OTHER BOOKS BY BRYAN R. COUPLAND:

*COME REST WITH ME – Experiencing Intimacy with Jesus through God's Rest*

Does Jesus Christ make any provision for His children today to not only experience His peace and rest, but also to enter into deeper intimacy with Him? *Come Rest with Me* answers these questions from Scripture, punctuated with real-life anecdotes that explain how Jesus can live His life through ours. The author also interviewed four missionary widows whose husbands were killed by guerrillas. These women tell how real God's rest is in the fiery furnace of trials.

*GROWING A WISE FAMILY – 100 Devotionals from the Book of Proverbs*

Are "family devotions" a thing of the past? Has the contemporary Christian family changed so much that getting all together for a half hour every day is completely out of the question? Family devotions *never* become old fashioned. The author and his wife had just such a daily time with their three children in their growing up years. All three are married with their own children and now have these valuable times together with their own families. *Growing a Wise Family* not only provides one hundred devotionals from the wonderful book of Proverbs in the Bible, but adds three questions *with answers* after each devotional to help parents facilitate these times. Don't sell your family short! Make plans to get together daily around God's Word!

WATCH FOR THE *THIRD VOLUME* OF THE "FAMILY DEVOTIONS TRILOGY" CALLED: *A FAMILY OF GRACE – 100 Devotionals from Galatians, Ephesians, Philippians, and Colossians.*